KT-466-117

Running – The Basics

This book is dedicated to my wife Halgard. For more than 30 years, she has inspired me to study the physiological and biomechanical basics of running. This work has taken up a large part of my free time, and I thank her not just for putting up with it, but also for helping me to transfer theory into practice.

Carl-Jürgen Diem
February 2004

Carl-Jürgen Diem

Running

– The Basics

Meyer & Meyer Sport

Original title: Grundlagen des Ausdauersports – Laufen
© Aachen: Meyer & Meyer, 2001
Translated by Heather Ross

British Library Cataloguing in Publication Data
A catalogue record for this book is available from the British Library

Diem, Carl-Jürgen:
Running – The Basics
Oxford: Meyer & Meyer Sport (UK) Ltd., 2004
ISBN 1-84126-139-4

© 2004 by Meyer & Meyer Sport (UK) Ltd.
Aachen, Adelaide, Auckland, Budapest, Graz, Johannesburg,
Miami, Olten (CH), Oxford, Singapore, Toronto
Member of the World
Sports Publishers' Association (WSPA)
www.w-s-p-a.org
Printed and bound by: FINIDR, s. r. o., Český Těšín
ISBN 1-84126-139-4
E-Mail: verlag@m-m-sports.com
www.m-m-sports.com

Foreword

The author of "Running – The Basics" is no ordinary man!

For Carl-Jürgen Diem, running is a central part of himself, of his life and it is also his trademark. Fun-Running rallies are the instrument of his passion – culminating in the Fun-Running department of the German Athletics Federation.

He does not stop at running – circumstances have also led to walking being integrated – and for running is examined in its theoretical form, examined in the fullest sense of the word.

He has progressed informally from being just a club coach to becoming a highly-paid lecturer, having taken advantage of every available educational opportunity in the subject areas concerned, while at the same time teaching them.

We are dealing with a self-taught training academic and sports physiologist. And he knows what he is talking about.

He shows considerable self-confidence and courage in this book, partly due to his long history of studying the subject matter, and the credibility he has with the running public as an insider, a runner himself.

Textbooks like this one are usually written by doctors and people who have studied sport in a formal way. In his work, the training-sience interpretation and message have a strong sports medicine emphasis – psychology is given less importance.

It is very impressive how the runner Diem, with his background, has assimilated and processed highly academic literature, which he extracts from intellectual books and "translates" for the runner. The all-terrain runner needs clear advice and does not want to be confused by scientific theories and can, if in doubt, take one side, reach his own conclusions and trust hypotheses at face value until he makes his final choice. He writes academically, in a way that is useful for the runner. Academics are pleased to recognise on reading how their teachings have reached someone who understands the subject. Diem also knows a thing or two about graphics!

Diem's book builds a bridge between strictly academic papers and the runner's need for accessible and user-friendly running advice.

Dr. Manfred Steinbach

1 Introduction

"Aren't there enough books about running on the market already?" many people interested in endurance events will ask. Publishers and authors say: "Yes, but...." The market offers an almost unmanageable number of running books and training guides of all kinds. There are also many books on sports medicine. Training guides often lack the (sports) medical basics, why you should train in one way and not another and the sports medicine books almost always lack an explanation of the effects of certain physical processes on training or competition.

This book forms a bridge between sporting activity and the physiological and biomechanical processes it causes. It should help coaches, trainers, instructors, teachers, but especially athletes, whether trained or beginners, telling them how to derive their own individual, efficient endurance training programme. The extent of this information gap is shown by the daily practice at grass roots and intermediate level. According to the motto "the more the better", training is often too intensive in terms of speed and/or volume. The opposite, that "less can be more", when loading is correct and a balance of training types is included in the training programme, is strongly promoted in this book. The positive effects of endurance training on the health and immune system are achieved by a well-balanced training programme, not a one-sided one.

As the number of runners who walk for reasons of age or injury at least sometimes is increasing steeply, the loading differences between running and walking are indicated in some chapters.

Each separate chapter is self-contained and they do not have to be read in the order they appear in the book. Also, when chemical formulae of the more complicated physiological processes are shown, no knowledge of chemistry or medicine is required. The chemical formulae are also graphic complements to the text. Medical terms are not totally dispensed with, but they are explained.

The basics of the cardio-vascular system, energy production and the biomechanical aspects of running are gone into in great detail, as they constitute the basis of an optimal training programme.

Among other main topics are:

▶ the possibilities and range of application of lactate and pulse-rate measurement
▶ the biomechanical aspects of the optimisation of strength transfer and the avoidance of overloading and injury
▶ the interrelationship and interdependency between endurance training on the one hand and coordination, mobility, speed and strength training on the other
▶ advice on the purchase of suitable running shoes and individual selection criteria to avoid buying the wrong shoes
▶ the importance of compensation exercises for the endurance athlete.

Further reading, in which the energy production process, muscle function, etc. are presented in more detail, is indicated where appropriate.

1.1　Definition of the Term 'Endurance'

In the teaching of motor function, i.e. the teaching of movement, there are five basic training forms, also called "main forms of motor loading" by Hollmann/Hettinger [38], which the author would like to supplement with a sixth (see also Chapter 5: "Coordination, Mobility, Speed and Strength Training"):

1. Coordination
2. Flexibility
3. Speed
4. Strength
5. Endurance
6. *Concentration*

Each of these basic forms should be worked on independently and specifically. No one form can compensate for another, but each one influences all the others. For example: strength training gives the athlete neither speed nor endurance, however he needs strength e.g. in the thighs if he wants to run uphill.

The terms 'coordination', 'flexibility', 'strength' and 'speed' are easily and clearly defined. Their interrelationship and interdependence with endurance training will be thoroughly examined in a corresponding chapter.

The term "endurance" covers very different abilities: the ability to watch TV, to sit in the pub, the ability of a politician to dodge unpleasant questions, etc. Endurance ability is needed by the ice-dancer for his five-minute freestyle routine just as much as by the downhill skier to reach the finish after his two-minute run.

This book deals with running, so the term **endurance running** should be defined more carefully. When preparing the schedule, it should be noted that a warm-up phase is a prerequisite both for optimal endurance training and racing (cf. Chapter 3.2.3 "Warming up, the correct Speed"), it should last from 30 to 120 minutes depending on the objective and it is not included in the training time.

In the technical literature, endurance is divided into periods:

▶ short distance   from 35 seconds to 2 minutes, e.g. 400 m and 800 m
▶ middle distance   from 2 to 10 minutes, e.g. 1,000 m to 3,000 m
▶ long distance   over 10 minutes.

In the specialist sports literature, long distance events are often further sub-divided into >10 minutes, >35 minutes and >90 minutes.

1.2 Reasons for Endurance Training

For popular runners and marathon runners the reasons are obvious: they need to do endurance training in order to achieve their goals. For fun runners, of which there are considerably more, there are completely different motivations (76, 77). It is important for coaches, instructors and teachers to acknowledge these. From a wide-ranging study by the author's hometown Running Club in Germany, the Darmstadt Running Club [18], in which 510 people participated, it emerged that "complement to work and everyday life", "being in the fresh air", "the joy of movement" were the main reasons for 60-70% of the respondents (cf. Figure 1). Between 30% and 60% of the respondents cited health and fitness. Therefore only 15% needed endurance training to improve their performance level and are to be categorised as competition level.

The analysis leads to another surprising result: 60-70% of participants, also those at a low performance level (speed v = 5-10 km/h), are happy with their level and do not wish to improve it. This attitude is difficult to accept for many athletes, and was likewise for the author, when he was a coach and trainer at the start of the Running Club.

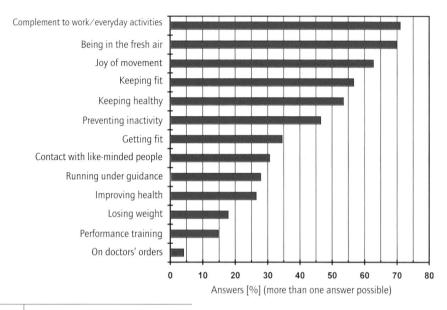

Figure 1: Reasons for participating at the Darmstadt Running club (by 510 participants).

1.3 Running Speed in Grass-roots Sport/Leisure Activities

The running speed at grass-roots level is considerably lower than can be expected from popular or marathon runners. For popular runners a speed of v = 11 km/h and for marathon runners v = 9 km/h are now the limits. The Darmstadt study featured above is sufficiently representative to be a general evaluation of grass-roots sport. It emerges from this study that in a one-hour training session a third of the "fun runners" run in the region of v = 5-7.5 km/h, v = 8-10 km/h and v>10.5 km/h (cf. Figure 2). The distribution is quite clear-cut between men and women, the latter fall mainly into the bottom part, the former into the top part.

For walkers, the slowest time is v = 5 km/h. The average is v = 6-7 km/h. The fastest rarely manage more than v = 8 km/h.

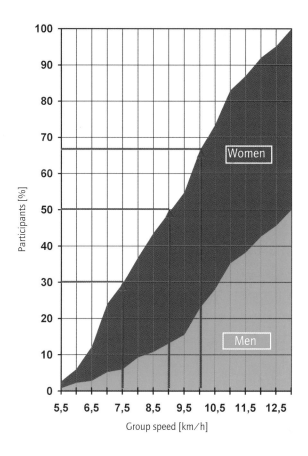

Figure 2: Participants in groups with running speed of v = 5.5 - 13 km/h in the Darmstadt Running Club [18]. All participants total 100%. The ratio of men to women is almost exactly 1:1. About 30% of participants run around v - 5.5 - 7.5 km/h, 50% at v = 5.5-9 km/h. Only a third of participants run at v = 10.5 km/h.

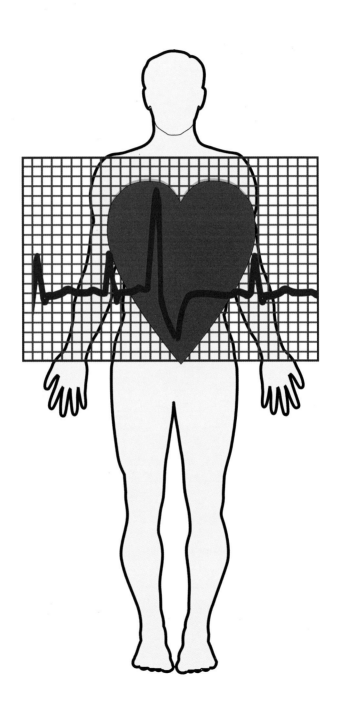

2 Anatomy of the Cardio-vascular System

The cardio-vascular system consists of a very sophisticated tubing system for the blood, measuring about 110,000 km (cf. Figure 3). Blood makes up 7-8% of the body weight, corresponding to 5-6 litres. The task of the blood is firstly the transport of:

- ▶ nutrients (carbohydrates, protein, fat)
- ▶ gases (oxygen, carbon dioxide)
- ▶ bio-catalysts (e.g. vitamins, hormones)
- ▶ metabolites (e.g. lactic acid, urea)
- ▶ salts (e.g. salt, calcium, magnesium)

and also to provide a water and temperature balance in the body (cf. Chapter 6.3.1 "Endurance Competitions in high Temperatures").

Blood consists of a liquid called plasma, in which blood cells swim. The plasma accounts for 55% and consists mainly of water. The blood cells (45%) are divided into red (erythrocytes), the white blood cells (leucocytes) and platelets (thrombocytes). The colour of the red blood cells comes from the haemoglobin that they carry. Oxygen is attached to them to be transported from the lungs to the blood vessels and muscles (cf. Chapter 2.5 "Breathing"). The amount of red corpuscles normally present is 5.5 billion per litre of blood in men and about 5 billion per litre of blood in women. The life expectancy of a blood corpuscle is only around 4 months, so that around 150 million new red blood corpuscles must be formed every minute.

The red blood corpuscle count is very important for the endurance athlete, as it constitutes the transporting capacity for oxygen. The count depends on the amount of oxygen present in the ambient air (see Chapter 2.5 "Breathing"). If this goes down, e.g. at heights of above 2000 m, additional red blood corpuscles are formed in order to maintain the amount of oxygen in the blood. This phenomenon is used in altitude training, exploiting the increased oxygen levels in the blood to produce better endurance performances (cf. Chapter 3.2.6 "Training Camps"). The effect is very limited timewise due to the short life-span of the red corpuscles and can be used effectively only by elite athletes. Another way of increasing the number of red corpuscles is the re-infusion of the athlete's own previously extracted blood to increase the amount of blood and thus the red corpuscle count; this is otherwise known as blood doping. The efficiency of this method is very controversial; blood thickening can give rise to adverse health reactions.

The vascular system (Figure 3) is divided into two parts, one with oxygen-enriched (arterial) blood and the other with blood that has given up its oxygen to muscles, organs and tissue (venous). 85% of the body's blood can be found in the venous area on the surface of the body and 15% in the deeper-lying arterial area. The oxygen-rich (arterial) blood is pumped by the left heart ventricle in to the arteries, the aorta (the start of the arterial area.) It flows in the large arteries to the brain, to the arms, legs and to each organ. There the arteries branch into fine, very elastic tubes (arterioles), which are spaced more or less close together according

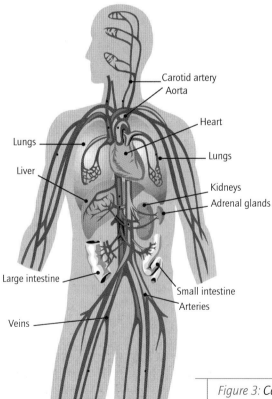

Carotid artery
Aorta
Heart
Lungs
Lungs
Liver
Kidneys
Adrenal glands
Large intestine
Small intestine
Arteries
Veins

Figure 3: Cardio-vascular system. Red– arterial part, blue – venous part.

to the supply needs of each individual muscle, organ or tissue. This arterial spacing controls the blood stream in the body and influences the blood pressure.

On the oxygen-weak (venous) side, fine, elastic tubes called venules discharge into large veins. The connections between the arterioles and venules are called capillaries. The capillary walls are porous, for the supply of the organs and muscles with oxygen and energy and the disposal of metabolites, e.g. carbon dioxide, lactic acid, etc. takes place in this area. Training increases the number of capillaries and thus the ability to supply oxygen and energy. Regular endurance training also trains the heart muscle, i.e. not only strengthens it, but also improves the capillary system, thus greatly reducing the consequences of a heart attack, as shown in Figure 9. The chances of survival and rehabilitation are increased up to 20 times. This is yet another benefit of endurance training.

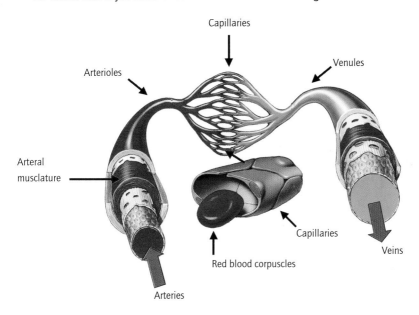

Figure 4: Capillary system.

While on the arterial side the blood is pushed towards the capillaries by the expulsion pressure of the heart muscle, on the venous side it must be sucked in by the heart. The sucking performance of the heart alone is not sufficient, so in the arm and leg areas the so-called muscle-vein-pump and vein valves help to prevent the blood from flowing backwards.

When the blood reaches the right ventricle, it continues to the lungs where the carbon dioxide (CO_2) it contains is exchanged for oxygen (O_2). It then flows back into the heart to be released back the circulation. (NB: In the section leading from the heart to the lungs, the connections are called arteries, even though they are carrying oxygen-depleted blood. Correspondingly, the connections from the lungs to the heart are called veins due to their backflow characteristic).

The diameter of the aorta is about D_A = 20 mm and the flow rate of the blood V_A = 40-70 cm/s. The arteries taper into the capillaries where the diameter is reduced to D_K < 0.025 mm. The blood flow rate must decrease en route by three decimal places to V_K = 0.05-0.1 cm/s. Only at this low flow rate is a sufficient contact time t = 0.3-0.4 s reached [48, 74] for a maximal exchange of oxygen, nutrients and metabolic waste products. If the flow rate is higher than this, the oxygen uptake of the blood in the capillaries is reduced by 60-40% as the contact time is too short.

2.1 Heart and Blood Pressure

The heart functions like a **"high performance two-circuit pump"**. Both circuits have a front and a main or pressure chamber, which work extremely hard on the left, arterial side (cf. Figure 5).

At rest, the heart has its own, autonomously-controlled stimulation and conduction system, from the sino-atrial node (the heart's cardiac pulse generator) starting continuously once the antechamber is electrically activated, thus squeezing the blood into the pressure chambers.

If these are full, the muscles of the pressure chambers are activated. They contract and force the blood out of the right chamber with about P_L = 20 into the lungs and at of the left chamber with about P_S = 130-180 mmHg, the upper (systolic) blood pressure, into the aorta. The blood pressure level results from the number of open and closed arterioles. It is labelled the afterload. In the first half of our lives, the aorta and the great arteries flowing into it hardly influence blood pressure at all. With increasing age, calcification and pathological changes can increase it.

After being squeezed out, the flagging heart muscle can stretch again and it simultaneously sucks blood from the veins and the lungs into the chambers. The elasticity of the aorta ensures that the blood pressure does not fall to zero in this phase, but instead maintains a value of about P_D = 70-90 mmHg. It is stretched in the squeezing phase, thus increasing its blood storing capacity.

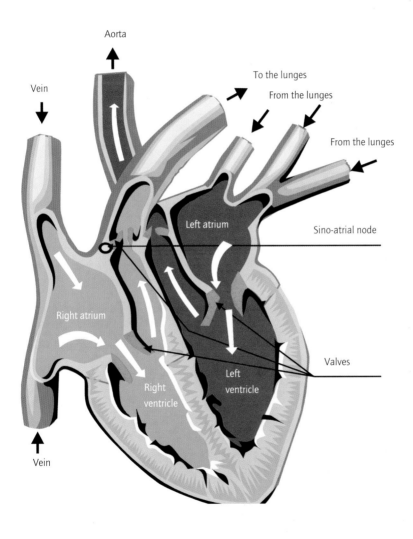

Figure 5: The heart, red: arterial part, blue: venous part.

In the full phase of the heart, the pressure coming from the heart to the Aorta and the elastic potential built up by stretching are released and part of the blood in the Aorta is forced out into the rest of the body. This stops blood pressure from sinking to zero, as one might expect. This pressure is called "lower pressure" (diastolic blood pressure) (it is often referred to in the literature as the *"elastic buffer function"* of the Aorta).

Under physical loading, systolic blood pressure increases up to a value of $P_S = 220$ mmHg, whereas the diastolic blood pressure P_D remains and should remain almost unchanged. In the arteriole area, blood pressure drops due to enlarged width to about 40 mmHg and that of the capillaries again drops to about 20 mmHg. During the backflow to the heart it is still only 2-4 mmHg in the superior vena cava.

There is a special cardio-vascular and blood-pressure regulation centre in the brain which has sensors (nerve endings) in the walls of the carotid and cerebral arteries which monitor blood pressure. A drop in blood pressure in these areas means a drop in the oxygen supply to the brain, which in extremis leads to the death of brain cells and to death.

A drop in blood pressure can be caused by shock, pooling of the blood in the stomach or thigh area due to psychologically-induced tension or anxiety or heavy blood loss due to injury.

The regulation centre does not, however, wait for a "tragedy" to happen, but instead reacts immediately to improve and restore the blood and oxygen supply to the brain. The best known way is by fainting, which forces the body into a horizontal position so that the blood no longer has to be pumped upwards, but can flow horizontally at low pressure from the heart to the brain.

At the same time the brain shuts down all the skeletal muscles so that the body collapses and also deals with external, mechanical injuries. This can also happen in a race, e.g. due to a fear of "not being able to keep up with the group". The author has experienced one such case directly, and he knows of two others.

Fainting is different from a cardio-vascular collapse in that the victim on the ground is certainly rather dazed, but he can immediately open his eyes normally, start to breathe deeply and stand up and walk. In both cases everyone should be vigilant, as first aid (heart massage, mouth-to-mouth resuscitation, calling an ambulance, etc.) may have to be carried out automatically under stressful conditions.

2.2 Systole, Diastole, maximal Heart Rate

The external supply of the heart muscle with blood and oxygen is only possible via both coronary arteries (Figure 6). In the blood output phase (systole), they are so severely constricted by the pressure effect of the heart muscle in the lower pericardium area that no blood and therefore no oxygen supply is possible during this time.

Blood only flows during the filling phase (diastole). The duration of both phases is varies according to the heart rate. If the heart rate increases, e.g. from 60 to 180 beats per minute, there is a shortening of the :

▶ systolic period insignificantly from $t_{S60} = 0.33$ s to $t_{S180} = 0.22$ s
▶ diastolic period greatly from $t_{D60} = 0.67$ s to $t_{D180} = 0.12$ s [71, 74],
   i.e. of almost 1/6 of the supply time (cf. Figure 7)

In young people, this does not normally present a problem. In the elderly on the other hand, when the arteries are clogged up and the supply to the organs and muscles drops due to the reduction in diffusion speed, it is crucial that the heart rate must not be raised too high while exercising. A temporary undersupply of oxygen leads to damage in the affected cells; in the heart muscle this can mean a heart attack.

The connection between age and maximal heart rate discovered by Hollmann/Hettinger [38] :

$$HR_{max} = 220 - age$$

thus gains an additional safety aspect: heart attack prevention. Older sports people, not just runners but also cyclists and cross-country skiers, who do not respect these limits but push their bodies too far, are running a high risk of a heart attack.

Figure 8 shows the theoretical HR_{max} – curve as well as the optimal endurance training zone $HR_{60-80\%}$ derived from it. The Hollmann-formula is very general, you can find out how to calculate your own maximal pulse rate more exactly in Chapter 3.2.2 "Heart Rate Monitoring". There you will learn that both positive health and optimal endurance training effects are only reached at 60-80% of the maximal performance speed.

A well-trained athlete is still not protected against a heart attack e.g. due to a blood clot (Figure 9), but his chances of survival are greater due to the increased level of capillary formation (up to 20 times more than an untrained person).

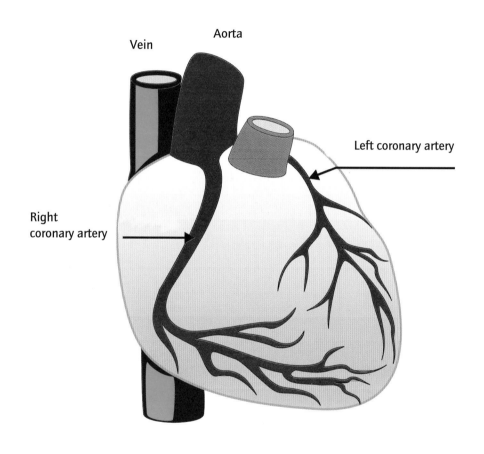

Figure 6: The heart with left (front wall) and right (rear wall) arteries.

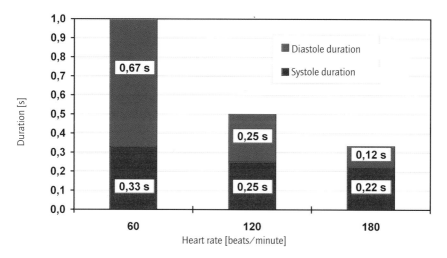

Figure 7: Connection between systole/diastole duration and heart rate.

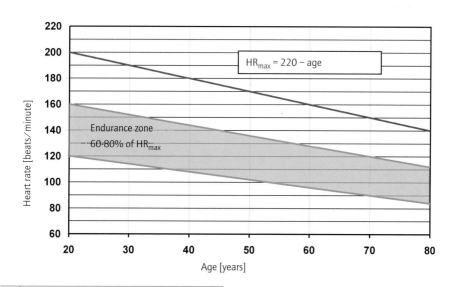

Figure 8: Maximal heart rate (HR_{max}) after Hollmann/Hettinger [38] and the 60-80% zone as optimal endurance training heart rate zone.

2.3 Heart Weight, Heart Size

The average weight of an untrained heart is M = 300 g (see Table 1, page 112). Endurance training increases the heart muscle mass up to M = 500 g. This means a simultaneous strengthening of the heart muscle. There are similar relationships for heart volume. The volume (V) increases in men (M) by V_M = 750 ml up to about V_M = 1,200 ml and in women (W) from V_W = 550 ml up to about V_W = 1,000 ml.

In terms of average bodyweight, the increase in volume is the same for women and men. The greater volume combined with the greater muscle strength lead to the desired higher blood production per heartbeat. At rest the heart rate therefore falls and under loading the increased amount of blood produced leads to improved endurance ability.

However, like every muscle, the heart muscle degenerates if training is reduced or ceased.

2.4 Heart Rate and Blood Circulation

Heart rate and blood production are affected both by the oxygen demand of the working muscles and organs and also by external emotional and visual stimuli (anxiety, fear, arousal, etc). At rest, control is maintained by the heart's own autonomous system. Under external emotional or visual stimuli, the "vegetative" nervous system (which controls and coordinates all functions of the inner organs) also intervenes with the sympathetic part as an activator (and with the "parasympathetic" part as buffer) in the control of heart rate and blood production.

The mental focussing on a forthcoming performance is a major emotional stimulus for the athlete (cf. Chapter 3.2.3 "Warming up – the correct Speed"). The heart rate rises, thus preparing for an increased oxygen and energy demand. The fine-tuning for the loading demand is controlled, e.g. by the change in ph value of the blood as a result of the accumulating metabolic waste products (cf. Chapter 3.1 "Obtaining Energy from Carbohydrates and Fats").

The oxygen requirement of the human body at rest – defined as resting pulse rate while still lying in bed in the morning – irrespective of training condition is, on average, V_{O_2} = 1 l O_2/min. The blood has an oxygen content of around V_{O_2} = 0.2 l per litre of blood: V_{rest} = 5 l blood/min is necessary to satisfy the oxygen

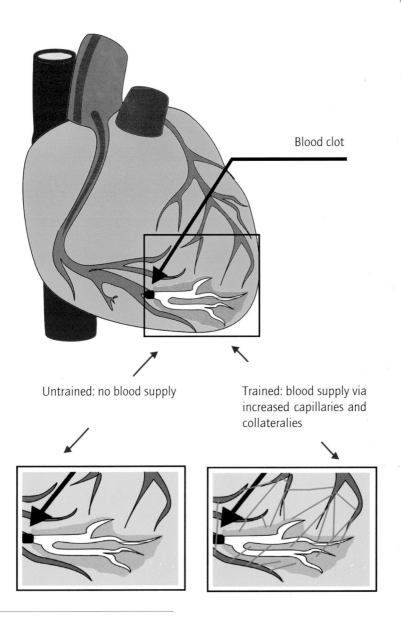

Blood clot

Untrained: no blood supply

Trained: blood supply via increased capillaries and collateralies

Figure 9: Through endurance training additional capillaries and collateralies are formed for a better supply to the heart muscle, which improve the possibilities and quality of survival in the case of a heart attack.

requirement at rest. The smaller heart of the untrained person requires about 70 beats per minute (resting heart rate HR_{rest}), as his stroke volume is about $V_{AU} = 70$ ml per heart beat. The bigger and stronger heart of the endurance trained athlete can cope with the blood requirement of $V_{rest} = 5$ l/min with only $HR_{rest} = 40\text{-}50$ beats/min, as the stroke volume at rest has increased to $V_{AT} = 100\text{-}125$ ml/heart beat. This represents an enormous economy of effort for the heart, which will be explained in detail below.

The blood available in the heart is $V = 5\text{-}6$ litres and can be increased by endurance training to $V = 6\text{-}7$ litres. The more blood available in the heart, the higher the red blood cell count, i.e. the greater its ability to transport oxygen.

If more muscle groups are used during a movement, the oxygen demand rises with both the volume and the work rate of the muscle groups concerned. The cardio-vascular system of an untrained and trained person react to this in very different ways.

Untrained:

► The increased oxygen demand is met mainly by an increase in heart rate and to a lesser extent by greater blood production, usually approximately a maximal $V_{U_{max}} = 120$ ml/heart beat, and at about $V_{U_{max}} = 24$ l/min (at $HR_{max} = 200$ beats/min). Heart rates are rapidly reached at which stroke volume sinks as the systolic phase is too short. At the same time, oxygen uptake decreases about 60-40% as the blood flows too fast through the capillaries (shortened contact time). For the same reason, a too-high breathing rate impairs oxygen uptake and carbon dioxide transfer in the lungs (cf. Chapter 3.1 "Obtaining Energy from Carbohydrates and Fats").

Trained:

► The trained athlete initially meets his increased oxygen demand by increasing stroke volume and secondly with an increase in heart rate. Through endurance training, a stroke volume of up to $V_{T_{max}} = 200$ ml/heart beat and up to $V_{T_{max}} = 40$ l/min (at $HR_{max} = 200$ beats/min) can be attained.

The additional capillaries in his muscles reduce the flow rate of the blood in the area of oxygen transfer, so that optimally an oxygen uptake rate of over 90% can be reached. This large oxygen supply in the working muscle enables the trained athlete to remain in oxygen balance even at substantially higher performance levels, unlike the untrained person (see Chapter 3.1 "Obtaining Energy from Carbohydrates and Fats").

The high oxygen consumption rate leads to a very slight oxygen residue in the venous blood. This increases the oxygen concentration gradient in the lung air sacs (alveolae) between the venous blood and the oxygen available there (oxygen partial pressure). At the same time, the trained athlete increases the number of active alveolae by breathing very deeply (cf. Chapter 2.5 "Breathing") and thereby also improves the oxygen and carbon dioxide exchange.

The slowing of the heart rate leads to an additional effect of improving the oxygen supply to the heart muscle by prolonging the diastolic phase (cf. Figure 7).

The oxygen and blood demand of the organs and muscles at rest is $V_{rest} = 1$ l O_2/min = 5 l blood/min. The demand of the individual organs and muscles is shown in Figure 10.

Intensive muscular effort, e.g. fast running, can increase the blood demand to $V = 25$ l blood/min. Figure 10 shows that this does not affect the requirement of the brain. At $V_{brain} = 0.8$ l blood/min it is independent of brain and bodily activity. The same goes for the kidneys. However, the blood supply to the digestive organs and the skin is noticeably reduced. The available blood is required either for digestion or the muscle supply, not both at the same time!

The blood distribution in the body is controlled by the vegative nervous system over the sympathetic nervous system by means of receptors. So-called α-receptors cut the blood supply for unnecessary skin, fatty tissue and organs; β_2-receptors open the energy and oxygen supply to the harder working muscles in the coronary area.

In the heart muscle β_1-receptors control the opening of the capillary area necessary for higher pumping output. Higher pumping performance is automatically linked to an increase in blood pressure. If this must be limited for reasons of health (high blood pressure), it can be regulated by taking beta-blockers. A restriction of output of the heart (the "engine") means a simultaneous restriction of overall physical activity. The taking of beta-blockers involves weighing up health benefits and a reduction of maximal productive efficiency.

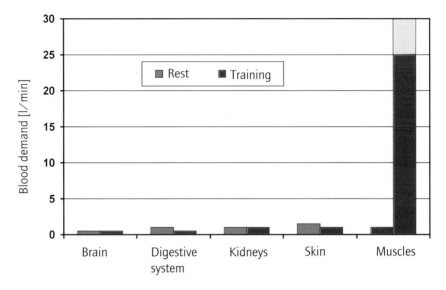

Figure 10: Blood demand in the body at rest and under maximal physical loading (training).

2.5 Breathing

The body has two different supply systems at its disposal. The first is in the stomach-intestine area for the intake of liquid and solid nutrition and the second in the lungs for the intake of oxygen. While people can survive three weeks without eating and up to three days without drinking, their oxygen supply must be guaranteed, as cells cannot survive more than about 3 minutes without oxygen.

Air breathed in from the atmosphere contains about 21% oxygen, about 78% nitrogen and about 1% other gasses. Exhaled air at rest still contains 16-17% oxygen and a 4% increase in carbon dioxide. The high amount of oxygen left serves to maintain a sufficiently high level of oxygen in the whole breathing area – and as a positive side effect it allows for mouth-to-mouth resuscitation to take place.

Breathing takes place in the upper and lower airways (Figure 11). The upper airway includes the nasal and pharyngeal areas, in which the inhaled air is warmed up, moistened, and cleaned of large particles of dirt. The air is heated to

37 °C (even from sub-zero temperatures), so that protective measures are only necessary when training in extreme conditions. The lower airway includes the larynx, with the vocal chords, the windpipe, and the bronchial tubes (wind-pipes in the lungs), which taper off into ever-smaller bronchioles (small wind-pipes) up to the alveoli (pulmonary alveoli and gas-exchange areas). The inner surfaces of the windpipe and the bronchial tube are lined with mucous glands and cilia, which continuously transport sticky particles in the mucous layer up to the larynx with rhythmic movements. Smoking, for example, considerably reduces this self-cleaning effect as it damages the cilia.

2.6 Air Pressure, partial Pressure

The pressure exerted upon us by the surrounding air is called **air pressure**. At sea level when the air is dry, air pressure exerts P_{air} = 760 mmHg. **Partial pressure** means the ratio to total pressure of the pressure of the proportion one of the individual gases contained in the ambient air. The partial pressure of oxygen (O_2) is, commensurate with its presence of about 21%, P_{O_2} = 760 * 21% = 160 mmHg.

In the airway from the nose and mouth through the bronchioles to the alveoli this oxygen partial pressure falls due to, among other things, the moistening of the air and the blending with carbon dioxide (CO_2) enriched exhaled air to P_{O_2} = 100 mmHg.

All gases, including air, oxygen and carbon dioxide, have the property of always moving from higher to lower concentrations and pressure areas, in order to maintain a concentration and pressure equilibrium. The gases important for the body are oxygen and carbon dioxide. Oxygen is necessary for the transfer of energy inside organ and muscle cells. Inside the cells, an oxygen partial pressure of $P_{O_2} \approx 1$ mmHg is assumed [71], i.e. between the oxygen available in the lungs ($P_{O_{2\,lungs}}$ = 100 mmHg) and the cells there is a great difference in pressure, which favours the transportation and the delivery of oxygen to the cells. Only very thin walls through which the oxygen can diffuse easily separate the alveoli and the surrounding capillaries.

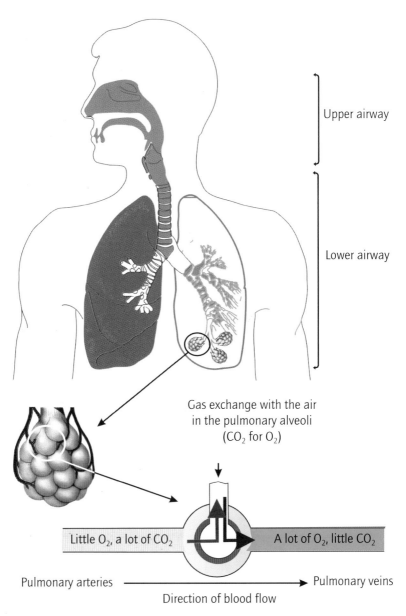

Upper airway

Lower airway

Gas exchange with the air
in the pulmonary alveoli
(CO_2 for O_2)

Little O_2, a lot of CO_2

A lot of O_2, little CO_2

Pulmonary arteries

Pulmonary veins

Direction of blood flow

Figure 11: Airways: upper area nasal and pharyngeal area: lower area: larynx, windpipe, bronchioles, pulmonary alveoli and gas exchange areas [7].

As oxygen is poorly water soluble, it is bound to haemoglobin (red blood cells) in the blood for transportation further. The binding of the oxygen to the haemoglobin is very fragile, thus facilitating the transfer to the oxygen-hungry organs and muscles. The transfer to the organs and between the capillaries and the muscle cells (cf. Figure 4) again takes place by diffusion.

Oxygen demand is generally low at rest; only part of the oxygen available in the arterial blood is required (the oxygen is not completely taken up), so that the venous blood that flows back to the pulmonary area can still contain oxygen with a partial pressure of up to $P_{O_2} = 40$ mmHg. Accordingly, the difference in pressure in the newly inhaled oxygen intake between the alveoli and the pulmonary capillaries is small.

The maximal amount of oxygen that can be supplied to cells depends on the flow rate of the blood in the capillaries. The contact time (t) must be $t = 0.3$ m/s. If the flow rate increases due to extreme loading, e.g. in a 400 m race or due to the low capillary capacity of the untrained person, oxygen uptake can drop to 40-60%.

Very fit endurance athletes can, however, still reach an oxygen uptake (VO_2 max) of up to 95% ($P_{O_2} < 10$ mmHg) even under extreme loading (e.g. marathon). This leads to a drop of pressure in the lungs, which in turn increases the diffusion rate of the oxygen and works together with the increased activity of the alveoli so that a maximal oxygen uptake in the blood is maintained.

In contrast to earlier theories, breathing is now no longer considered to be a performance-limiting factor for aerobic endurance performance [38]. Limiting effects can be too shallow breathing or smoking, when only some of the available alveoli are activated for gas exchange (O_2, CO_2), or when alveoli are deactivated through the accumulation of tar deposits due to smoking. The oxygen uptake in the capillaries in the area of the muscle cells is vital for endurance efficiency.

The gas carbon dioxide (CO_2), a metabolic waste product in the energy transfer process in the muscles, is unlike oxygen, very water soluble and can be dissolved in the venous blood and easily transported on to the lungs. There it is diffused via the alveoli into the bronchioles and then exhaled.

2.7   Breathing Volume, Breathing Capacity

The gas volume inhaled or exhaled during the breathing cycle is termed **tidal volume.** At rest it is about 0.5 l and it can be increased to up to 3 l by intensive physical activity, about 50% of the lung capacity. **Lung capacity** is the volume that can be maximally exhaled after maximally inhaling. Despite maximal exhaling there is always some air left in the lungs, the **residual volume.** The lung capacity and the residual volume together give the **total capacity.** The total capacity of the lungs is predetermined in detail for each of us and cannot be increased by breathing or endurance training.

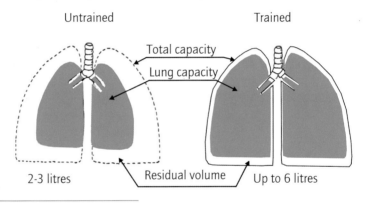

Figure 12: Schematic illustration of the total and lung capacity and the residual volume of untrained and trained people.

The lung capacity, however, can be maximised by deep and deliberate strong exhaling, i.e. by stomach/breast breathing instead of shallow breast breathing only (Figure 13). The deeper you exhale, the deeper you automatically inhale afterwards, i.e. deep exhaling is the precondition for deep inhaling.

Hence the recommendation that under loading or stress one should always concentrate on breathing deeply. Deep breathing (out) automatically leads to a reduction in the breathing rate and also to a reduction in heart rate and stress!

Certain breathing-stride patterns (e.g. six strides exhaling, four strides inhaling) make little sense in the light of current knowledge. The beginner improves and changes his breathing technique with growing endurance ability, on uneven surfaces breathing must be adapted to the changing load and a very fit endurance runner automatically adopts a breathing-stride pattern on the flat.

Breast breathing   Stomach/breast breathing

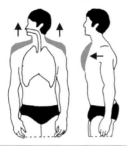 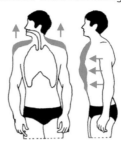

Figure 13: Comparison of chest breathing and chest and stomach breathing.

During inhalation, only part of the inhaled gas volume reaches the alveoli area in which gas exchange takes place. About 150 ml of each breath remain in the mouth, pharynx, larynx, windpipe and bronchial areas. As no gas exchange takes place in these areas, they are known as **dead space**. This value is more or less constant, i.e. the greater the amount of air inhaled, the smaller the ineffective dead space component of the lung capacity.

The **minute volume** is the volume that can be inhaled in one minute. It is the product of **breathing rate** – breaths per minute – multiplied by **tidal volume**. At rest, an adult breathes about 15 times per minute and the frequency can rise to 40-50 breaths if necessary. There is an optimum minute volume between breathing rate and tidal volume. If the breathing rate is too fast, the tidal volume drops. The smaller it gets, the more the gas exchange in the lungs is reduced, i.e., the oxygen content falls. At the same time, the alveoli area at the bottom of the lungs is no longer used in the gas exchange since breathing has become shallower. Both lead to a reduction in the oxygen component of the blood.

For many years, great importance was attached to finding the tidal rate, the lung capacity, the minute volume and the total capacity as components of the performance diagnosis. We now know that breathing is not a performance-limiting factor and is affected by many uncontrollable external factors. That is why such diagnostic tests are now only carried out at elite level.

Nose Clips are supposed to improve breathing through the nose. The improvements claimed by the advertisements should not be trusted, as there is, as yet, no scientific evidence for them. It is true that under intensive physical loading the breathing rate rises and, under these conditions, most people breathe through their noses as well as their mouths. When elite athletes wear these products, it is often just for endorsement purposes.

3 Basics of Energy Production and practical Consequences

The aim of this chapter is to explain the complex processes of energy production so clearly that they can be understood even without previous chemical or medical knowledge and can be transferred to individual training conditions. This required a lot of simplification. Readers who want to know more about this topic should refer to the further reading.

The formulae and diagrams used should be a graphic complement to the text, to facilitate understanding of the physical processes. The chemical structure formulae show where the energy potential is in a molecule and which atoms the molecule can be split into and what it means when incorrect training leaves energy potential unused.

The available energy reserves are normally completely adequate for short and middle distance requirements. In these short duration loads, the strength and speed of the athlete are crucial, as is his ability to deal with the metabolic waste products produced under these mostly very intensive loads. In the endurance category, however, success depends on an optimal utilisation of available energy reserves.

The energy production process can be compared to a nuclear power station, where energy is freed by splitting atoms. In the body, molecules are split into their constituent parts, thereby freeing energy that the body can use. It is a bonding energy that holds the atoms together inside the molecule. This means that every binding site between two atoms inside a molecule provides energy potential. The more binding sites there are, the greater the energy potential of the molecule.

Carbohydrates and fats (in the form of fatty acids) ingested with food serve as energy suppliers to the muscles. Protein is the third main nutritional component, 99% of which is used as building material for cells and 1% of which is used for energy production. This latter process is used as an emergency last resort if carbohydrates or fats are lacking (under nutrition).

As the conditions for this are not present for us, this context will not be dealt with further. Alongside carbohydrates and fats, the body also needs auxiliary substances such as enzymes, minerals and vitamins for the regulation of the processes.

The structure formulae in Figure 14 show how much energy is contained in a carbohydrate molecule and a fat molecule. The binding sites in which the binding energy is stored are shown as "blue". Those carbohydrate and fat molecules consisting of only three atoms break down during the splitting process to liberate energy into their components:

▶   carbon (C)
▶   hydrogen (H)
▶   oxygen (O)

The accumulated carbon and hydrogen atoms must be disposed of from the cells. This "disposal" and the binding of the hydrogen atom are the main tasks here. Disposal takes place by binding it to oxygen. Since there are few oxygen atoms available inside the carbohydrate and fatty acid molecules, oxygen must be brought in from outside. This takes place in the bloodstream in the lungs after inhaling. The necessary amount of oxygen depends upon the work intensity of the muscles, i.e. the number of the carbon and hydrogen atoms accumulated following the splitting process.

Under very high loading, e.g. sprinting, fast-pace running, uphill running, or sudden loading changes, not all the accumulated hydrogen atoms can be connected to the available oxygen, even under optimal conditions. The muscle cells must go into oxygen debt and switch to an inefficient alternative method of energy supply. This method allows high performance, but only for a short time, as the metabolic waste products so produced are only absorbed in limited quantities. There are a total of three ways in which the body can produce energy, and it is vital that an endurance athlete understands them. Which method can be used depends on the corresponding oxygen supply in the muscle cells:

▶   too little oxygen
▶   sufficient oxygen
▶   oxygen surplus

Each method, and their importance for the runner, are presented in the following chapters.

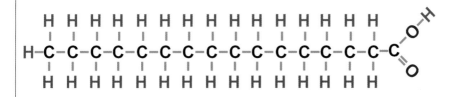

Figure 14: Chemical structure of glucose and palmitic acid (green connecting lines
= potential binding energy).

ATP – the body's "energy currency"

Energy is necessary for all physical functions. The electrical energy obtained from the splitting of carbohydrate and fatty acid molecules cannot be used directly, but must be made available with the help of a "go-between", i.e. Adenosine tri-phosphate (ATP).

This very complicated substance has the advantage that it is used as the universal and sole energy provider, independently of where it is required in the body, in the brain, the muscles, the organs etc. Energy production takes place, as already described in Chapter 3 "Basics of Energy Production", by the production of released electrical binding energy. Adenosine-**tri**-phosphate (ATP) splits off the third phosphate group, forming free energy potential, adenosine-**di**-phosphate and a phosphate residue (Figure 15).

According to the law of energy conservation, energy cannot be lost. For the body, this means that one part of this electrical energy is held back to be used later in this form. Another part is converted into heat, which serves to maintain body temperature, and to raise it during the warm-up phase.

Despite these central roles of ATP, the individual muscle cells have such minimal ATP stocks that they can only perform two or three contractions with them. To allow further contractions (movement – strides for the runner), immediate re-synthesis (regeneration) of ATP from ADP is necessary, i.e. the separated phosphate residue must be reconnected electrically to the ADP. As a first stage, the energy needed to do this can be obtained instantaneously from creatine phosphate (CP), allowing about six more contractions.

For all further contractions, i.e. those beyond these 8-9 strides, the body must split carbohydrates, fats and fatty acids. The re-synthesis of ATP into ADP now takes place with the aid of the electrical binding energy (E) released by this splitting process.

The chemical structures (Figure 14) of a carbohydrate molecule (glucose) and a fatty acid (palmitic acid) should show how much potential binding energy (= green connecting lines) is available in each molecule.

AdenosineTriPhosphate (ATP)
Splitting point at energy production ADP + P_1

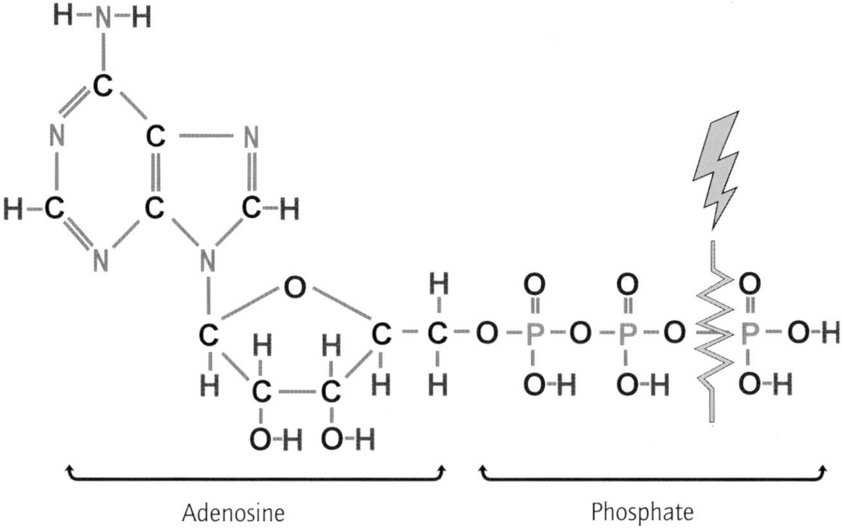

Adenosine

Phosphate

*Figure 15: Adenosine-**tri**-phosphate is the principal energy supplier for energy-using processes in the human body. The energy is formed from the splitting off of the last phosphate group (P_1) of ATP. Energy potential, Adenosine-**di**-phosphate (ADP) and a phosphate residue are formed. The energy potential is used in the muscle cells to tense the myosin molecules (cf. Chapter 4.2.2 ("Muscle Structure and Function"), to allow for the rolling movement required for contraction after their heads have been attached to the actin filaments [49, 71].*

3.1 Obtaining Energy from Carbohydrates and Fats

Figure 16 shows the diagram of a muscle cell with the most important components for energy production during muscle contraction. The supply of the muscle cells with the material necessary for this process, e.g. carbohydrates, fatty acids, protein, enzymes, oxygen, electrolyte, occurs via the arterial blood in the arteries; the removal of the "waste products" CO_2, H_2O, lactic acid etc., via the venous blood in the veins.

The so-called muscle power stations (mitochondria) are particularly important for the runner, as the oxygen-supply based processes for longer-term energy production can only take place here. Endurance training can increase their number by about 15-20%, thereby also improving related oxygen-dependent performance ability [40].

Energy can be produced from carbohydrates, due to their own high oxygen content (Figure 14), both with and without sufficient oxygen supply. For energy production from fatty acids, a high oxygen supply is necessary. To this end, the three following metabolic methods are identified:

▶ without sufficient oxygen supply: only one single splitting of a carbohydrate molecule = **anaerobic carbohydrate metabolism**
▶ with sufficient oxygen supply: one complete splitting of a carbohydrate molecule = **aerobic metabolic metabolism**
▶ high oxygen supply: complete splitting of fatty acids = **aerobic fat metabolism**

(aerobic = with oxygen; anaerobic = without oxygen)

3.1.1 Anaerobic Carbohydrate Metabolism

Carbohydrates in the form of glucose and glycogen (from glucose-unit containing macromolecules) feed the muscle cells via the arteries. They are also in reserve in deposits between the muscle cells or available for immediate use in deposits inside the muscle cells [38]. Endurance training can actually increase carbohydrate deposits by up to a maximum of 20%.

The first splitting of the glucose molecules takes place in the muscle cells, but still outside the muscle power stations (mitochondria). This is a four-step process that

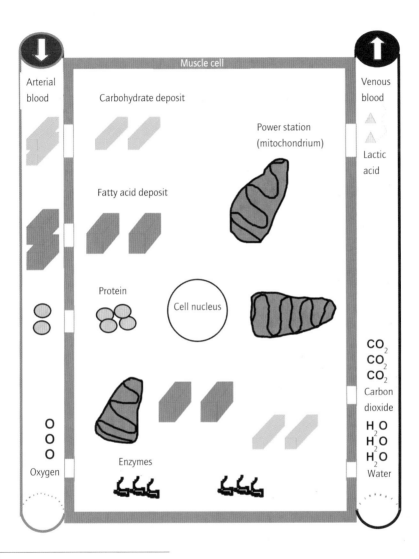

Figure 16: Diagram of the muscle cell with the muscle power stations *(mitochondria), in which aerobic energy production takes place. Carbohydrate (glycogen) and fatty acid deposits are stored in the muscle cells. The number of mitochondria and the size of the deposits depend on the training condition of the runner.*

is mainly regulated by enzymes [8, 25, 35, 47, 74]. We shall not go into the complex details of this process here as they are not necessary to understand the energy production process.

Energy is likewise required to split the ring-shaped glucose molecule (one ATP – in Figure 17 represented by the violet thunderbolt.). During the split, however, two new ATP are formed, leaving one available for the next muscle contraction.

Along with both products of the split, pyruvic acid, four hydrogen atoms also accumulate (2 x H_2). This hydrogen must be attached to so-called hydrogen carriers (NAD+ in Figures 17, 19 and 20 symbolised by ⌣) and transported to the mitochondria. There the hydrogen and oxygen – provided there is free oxygen available in the breathing chain – are combined as water and released into the venous blood.

The actual oxygen supply thereby regulates the number of free hydrogen carriers. If the level of effort in one muscle increases, so more hydrogen builds up due to the increased splitting, and it must be removed by free hydrogen carriers. The increased oxygen supply required for this must first go through various processes – as far as the work intensity allows this. Conclusion: after only a few splits, no free hydrogen carriers are available due to oxygen debt.

Further contractions (strides) are still possible though. The muscle cells must get rid of the accumulated hydrogen and now use the possibility of attaching the hydrogen to both split products (pyruvic acid) (Figure 18). Lactic acid is formed (lactate). This process is called anaerobic carbohydrate metabolism, as it takes place without oxygen.

The body must always use this method when a muscle starts to work and the intensity of effort is increased and the necessary oxygen supply is not (yet) sufficient. The lactic acid is released into the venous blood circulation where it acidifies the blood. This acidification of the blood then triggers heavy breathing via the central nervous system (CO_2 – oxygen exchange) and heart activity, in order to increase the oxygen supply in the working muscle by increasing the blood supply (cf. Chapter 3.2.3 "Warming-up – the correct Speed").

During **anaerobic** carbohydrate metabolism, the carbohydrate molecule is only split once, i.e. only 5% of its binding energy can be used. The other 95% of the binding energy remains unused in the lactic acid and is no longer available to the runner's working skeletal muscles during the training session or race. The heart

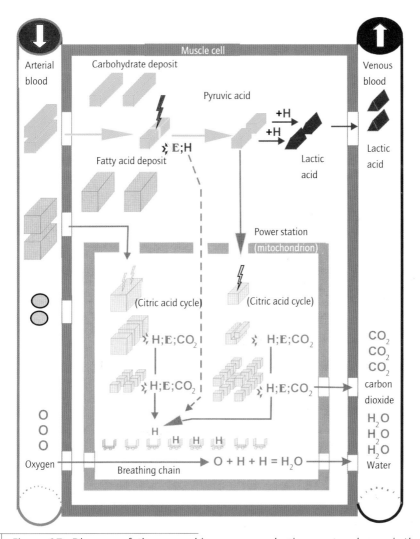

Figure 17: Diagram of the anaerobic energy production process by a single splitting of a carbohydrate molecule.

Top of figure: The first splitting of a carbohydrate molecule (glycogen) takes place after its activation ⚡ outside the power station. Two molecules of pyruvic acid are formed. At the same time, binding energy E and hydrogen H are released. Since all hydrogen carriers ⨆ in the power station are occupied (for the time being), the hydrogen atoms H_2 must be attached to the pyruvic acid molecules. Lactic acid (lactate) is formed and released into the venous circulation.

45

Glucose ($C_6 H_{12} O_6$) – splitting

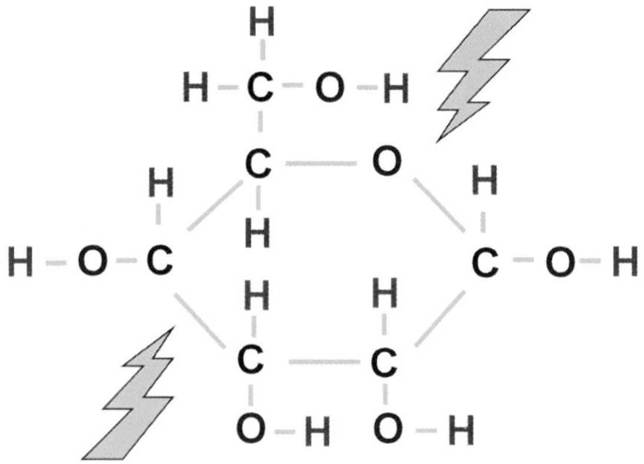

2 x pyruvic acid (CH_3-CO-COOH) +2 x H_2

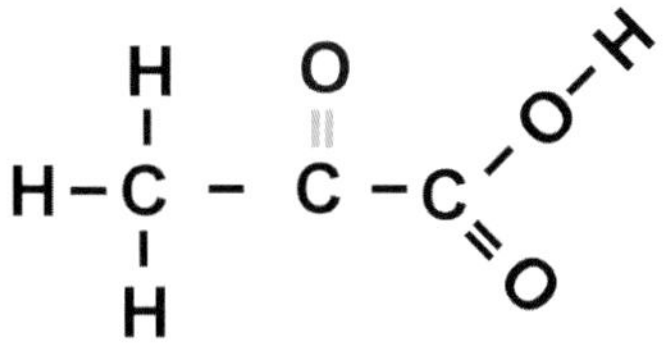

If oxygen supply is sufficient, further splitting, otherwise attachment to H_2, i.e. lactic acid formation (CH_3-CHOH-COOH)

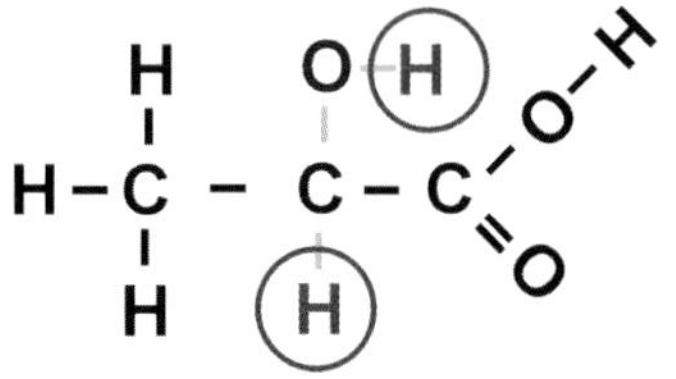

Figure 18: Chemical structure of glucose, pyruvic acid and lactic acid.

muscle is an exception. Compared to the skeletal muscles it contains a very high number of muscle power stations (mitochondria), thus a healthy heart possesses a sufficient number of these power stations. It can even use up to 50% of the lactic acid to generate energy.

That is why this extremely uneconomical form of energy production is only suitable for short bursts of activity, e.g. sprints or as the transition during the warm-up phase. Even nowadays, it is still astonishing how often endurance athletes, usually training alone, can be observed beginning and continuing every training session at too high an intensity (too fast) due to incorrect training ideas.

In this way, your limited carbohydrate deposits are emptied very rapidly (by a factor of 19) – after about 30-60 minutes for a runner – without really using them. The energy-containing lactic acid arrives via the blood circulation in the liver, where it is converted into carbohydrate within the next 24 hours.

A further disadvantage is that the muscle power stations (mitochondria) become damaged by too high lactate concentrations, thereby reducing both the number of hydrogen carriers and the possibility of binding hydrogen to the breathing chain [52].

3.1.2 Aerobic Carbohydrate Metabolism

The transition from anaerobic to aerobic carbohydrate metabolism is not only blurred but also variable. It depends on the oxygen supply present in every muscle power station (mitochondrion). If enough oxygen is available to take the hydrogen-loaded hydrogen carriers (NADH) and to bind them with water (H_2O) in the breathing chain, the pyruvic acid can diffuse into the muscle power stations and there be split until the last binding in the citric acid cycle (Figure 19). If loading intensity is increased, e.g. by accelerating or running uphill, energy production automatically reverts to the anaerobic method.

The choice of the correct running speed (loading intensity) is vital for the question of how fast the transition is made from anaerobic to aerobic carbohydrate metabolism. Optimally, a preliminary balance between oxygen demand and oxygen supply can be reached after about 20-30 minutes. This allows energy utilisation to rise to about 90-95%, i.e. a factor of 18-19 compared to the anaerobic metabolism, a fundamental pre-condition for all endurance performances.

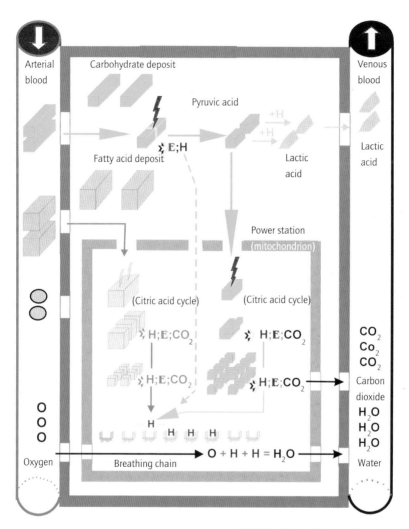

Figure 19: *Diagram of aerobic energy production by complete splitting of a carbohydrate molecule in the muscle power station (mitochondrion). Centre right: If there are enough hydrogen acceptors* ⊔ *free after the first splitting of carbohydrate molecules, the pyruvic acid is transported to the muscle power station and there broken down again in several stages in the citric acid cycle until it is split completely. Every splitting yields energy E. The accumulated hydrogen H is attached with oxygen O to form water H_2O, and the accumulated carbon C is attached to carbon dioxide CO_2.*

3.1.3 Aerobic Fat Metabolism

The transition from aerobic carbohydrate to fat metabolism is just as blurred as that of anaerobic to aerobic carbohydrate metabolism. It can be different from one muscle power station to another, depending on the oxygen supply. The splitting of fatty acid molecules is only possible inside the muscle power stations (Figure 20). This process requires around 15% more oxygen than the aerobic carbohydrate metabolism, as fatty acids contain more water and carbohydrate molecules which are used for binding. Fat metabolism is the real endurance metabolism. As explained above, while the carbohydrate stocks in the body are very limited, and can only be increased a little, the body has almost unlimited fat reserves.

To be able to access the body's fat reserves for energy production, the fats must be broken down into fatty acids. This process is only activated though when the fatty acids have preferably been fully exhausted in every training session. The more regularly they are used up, the more the formation of new fatty acids is stimulated. In this way not only is fat broken down, but at the same time the required fatty acid deposits are enlarged, since the body is continually trying to set up bigger reserves.

A further advantage of the endurance trained athlete is that, due to their superior oxygen consumption (more arterioles, slower flow rate of blood) and their well trained fat metabolism, the change from aerobic carbohydrate to fat metabolism takes place considerably sooner, thereby conserving valuable carbohydrates that can be used in the sprint finish of a race, for example.

This process should explain why endurance can only be achieved by endurance training in the fat metabolism. Peak performances in endurance sports, e.g. marathon or triathlon, can only be achieved with an optimally activated fat metabolism and very large fat deposits.

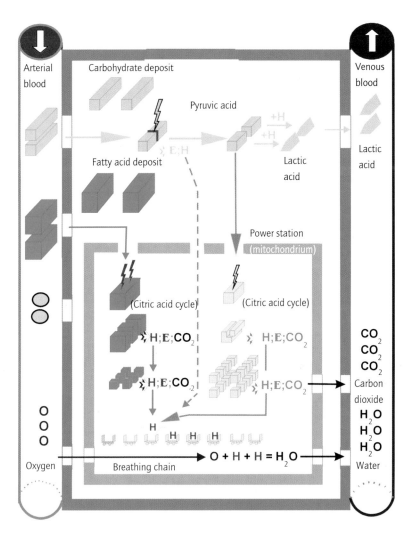

Figure 20: Diagram of aerobic energy production from fatty acids. Centre left: the fatty acids can only be split in the muscle power station (mitochondrion) after their activation. This automatically requires both free hydrogen carriers and at the same time a 15% higher oxygen supply, as fatty acid molecules contain more oxygen and carbon dioxide than carbohydrates. At every stage of the splitting process, energy E is released. The accumulated hydrogen H is combined with oxygen O to form water H_2O, the accumulated carbon C forms carbon dioxide CO_2.

Figure 21 shows the energy ratio during endurance training, at optimal running speed [64]. To achieve appreciable fatty acid ratios, long (at least 60 minutes) training sessions are necessary, which must be run slowly, i.e. at a maximum of 80% of maximal performance ability.

It also holds true for the fat metabolism that if the load is increased above the current oxygen supply, the energy production automatically changes back to aerobic – or even to the anaerobic carbohydrate until hyperlactatemia. How rapidly this process can kick in can be observed in the Olympic Games marathon in Seoul and Sydney. There the leading runner increased the pace at 39 km and tried to shake off his opponents. This seemed to be successful at first, but later he was not only not able to maintain the increased pace, but was running so slowly (hyperlactatemia?), that he was powerless to stop his opponent from passing him to take Olympic gold.

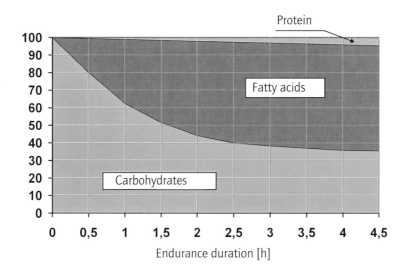

Figure 21: Energy ratios during endurance training under optimal running conditions.

3.2 Methodical Setting of optimal Training Speed

The knowledge of one's own optimal and training pace is a pre-requisite for efficient endurance training. Only the runner who trains at the optimal loading intensity can optimally increase his endurance ability and thereby improve his fitness, obtain positive health effects and a highly activated immune system. Basic research into this was carried out by Hollmann [34, 35] De Marées [48], among others, in the 60 s and 70 s. At that time, the transfer of the findings only benefited a few elite athletes in sports medicine institutes equipped with facilities for lactate (= lactic acid, more precisely the salt of lactic acid) and heart rate measurement. The general recommendations, e.g. *"pulse rate of 130"* or *"training pulse rate = 180 minus age"* were in fact published in all the training guidebooks, but their practice was the exception rather than the rule.

The combination of lactate and heart rate measurement is also still unavoidable nowadays, in scientific research or in performance tests on the world's best athletes. According to experiments carried out in the meantime [20, 23, 52], heart rate measurements are sufficient for competitive and fun runners. Heart rate monitors are on the market in all price ranges and specifications. In Chapter 3.2.1 "Lactate Measurement" below, the basics of lactate and heart rate measurement are explained and in Chapter 3.2.2 "Heart Rate Monitoring" several examples are given of the implementation of heart rate measurement in daily practice.

3.2.1 Lactate Measurement

As described above in detail, lactate is formed during every muscle action where insufficient oxygen is present, which is undesirable during endurance training and racing. In the warm-up phase, however, it is both unavoidable and necessary. Hence the motto:

> As much as necessary, as little as possible

for the endurance training goal is training in fat metabolism. The blood lactate content during or after a training session clearly shows in which metabolic zone training was carried out, i.e. anaerobic or aerobic carbohydrate or fat metabolism.

To measure lactate values, a droplet of blood is taken either from the earlobes or the finger tips. For photometric lactate measurement it can be dropped onto a test strip (similar to blood sugar measurement) or in a test solution. The author prefers blood to be taken from the finger tips, where the testee can watch the process. A new, sterile needle must be used for each blood extraction. The extraction point must be clean and sweat-free otherwise readings are not accurate. For the test strip method, a small, handy measuring kit was available from 1994-99 (Accusport, from the company Hestia/Boeringer Mannheim), which was very good for trial tests. For lactate measurement in test solutions, laboratory equipment is necessary.

A unit of lactate value (L) is given in millimol per litre (mmol/l). Values between L = 0.5 and L = 1.0 mmol/l correspond to normal daily activity. For aerobic training in the fat- and carbohydrate metabolism, it is up to L = 4.0 mmol/l. Values higher than this reflected anaerobic metabolism. The value L = 4.0 mmol/l was up to now designated the aerobic/anaerobic threshold [29, 30]. This limit value is not identical for every runner, that is why it is more appropriate to talk of a transition zone and to extend the aerobic/anaerobic threshold to L = 3 – 5 mmol/l.

To train in fat metabolism, the lactate value must be L ≤ 2.5 mmol/l [29]. Neumann [52, 53] now even recommends remaining below L ≤ 2 mmol/l.

The training zones are divided into types of running and lactate value as follows (cf. Figure 22):

L < 1.5 mmol/l   :   aerobic regeneration training

L = 1.5 – 3.0 mmol/l :   aerobic endurance training

L = 3.0-5.0 mmol/l   :   aerobic/anaerobic transition (threshold)

L > 5.0 mmol   :   anaerobic interval training

Even an optimal warm-up cannot prevent lactate formation, for example in a 100 m race already after about 20 m [9] and reaches extreme values in 400 m runners of up to L = 25 mmol/l. The decline in performance level associated with this hyperlactatemia can be observed in many 400 m runners over the last 50 m, when they run slower and slower and are almost standing still at the finish. All coaches and trainers in charge of children and young people should beware of these high lactate values. The lactate tolerance of these age groups is lower than adults as their body mass is lower! Middle distance races are particularly hard for these age groups and require a thorough warm-up, which is very rarely carried out.

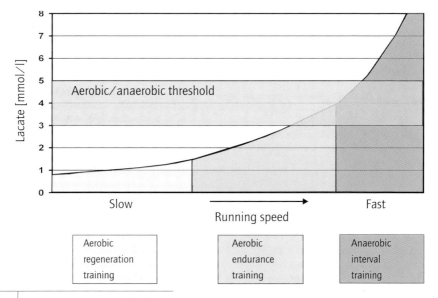

Figure 22: Lactate values for aerobic/anaerobic training zones.

World-class marathon runners reach the finish with L = 2-2.5 mmol/l, thus supporting the theory that such endurance performances are only possible in the fat metabolism. If the anaerobic/aerobic threshold is crossed, e.g. because of a too high starting speed or a sharp increase in speed during the race, the result is an increased energy withdrawal from the limited carbohydrate deposits for the inefficient energy production in the anaerobic carbohydrate metabolism, that can soon even result in hyperlactatemia (cf. Chapter 3.1.1 "Anaerobic Carbohydrate Metabolism").

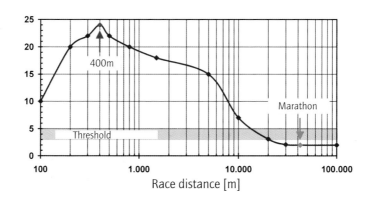

The connection between load (running speed) and lactate formation is not linear, but runs exponentially (see Figure 22). In Figure 24 sample curves are shown that are standardised for the target lactate value of L = 2 mmol/l (•) for various endurance performance abilities. The runners should exhibit a maximal lactate value of L = 2 mmol/l at the end of their training session (e.g. after one hour) at the predetermined load (optimal running pace). The lactate formation here is very strongly dependent on the endurance condition of the athlete, i.e. for one runner it is a speed of v = 6 km/h, another it is v = 10 km/h or v = 13 km/h. The worse the training condition, the sooner lactate formation starts; the fitter the athlete, the faster they can run before lactate formation causes hyperlactatemia.

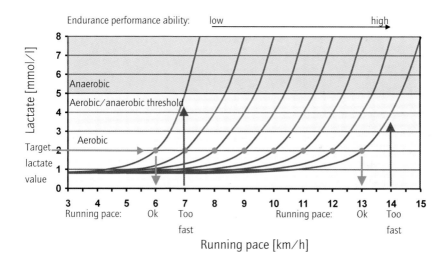

Figure 23: (left page) Lactate values for various race distances (half-logarithmic presentation).

Figure 24: The connection between load (running speed) and lactate formation is not linear, but runs exponentially. The sample curves for various endurance performance abilities are standardised for a target lactate value of L = 2 mmol/l (•), which the runner should exhibit at the end of their training session at the predetermined training speed. The curves show both the increase or decrease of the lactate value and in which energy production zone the athlete is in, when they deviate from their planned speed and from their optimal training intensity.

Readers can draw up their own curves. From these curves they can then learn what happens when they run faster or slower than the desired running speed (running speed at L = 2.0 mmol/l). If they run at v = 7 km/h instead of the desired v = 6 km/h, the lactate value rises from L = 2 mmol/l to L = 4.5 mmol/l, thereby reaching the upper limit of the aerobic/anaerobic threshold area, i.e. their endurance training is not in the fat metabolism, but their energy is produced partly aerobically, partly anaerobically from carbohydrates. The same thing happens to the runner who runs at v = 13 km/h instead of 12 km/h.

Individual lactate performance curves are determined in the so called graded lactate test and should always be carried out in a sport-specific way, i.e. running for runners, on a bicycle for cyclists, etc. When running, it is preferable that the test should be carried out on a treadmill rather than on a track in the countryside, as the running speed can be determined accurately and the overall conditions are easily reproduceable. The proven method is to run for four or five minutes at each respective pace (loading level) and to rest for one minute for blood withdrawal. This test is completed by heart rate monitoring running in conjunction with permanent recording. When trying to load to full capacity, heart rate monitoring is an essential safety and precautionary measure. With the S-series from POLAR, it is now also possible to do without loading to full capacity, as this heart rate monitor allows the HR_{max} to be determined in a special process. (see following chapter).

3.2.2   Heart Rate Monitoring

It is too time-consuming to take a lactate reading at every loading and speed change. Heart rate monitoring is a good alternative. On the one hand there is a clear correlation between heart rate and lactate value and on the other hand heart rate monitoring is always simple to carry out. Also, the heart rate reacts very sensitively within a few seconds to every loading change, i.e. both to an increase or decrease in loading (Figure 25). The heart rate, unlike the lactate value, rises in an almost linear fashion right up to maximal loading.

(N.B.: In the testing process developed by Conconi "Heart Rate depending on Running Velocity", there should be a slight blip in the otherwise linear curve in the aerobic/anaerobic threshold area. Since the test results are very much dependent on the test conditions and difficult to reproduce due to insufficient standardisation, we will not explore this method further.)

There are two possible methods for the plotting of the heart rate in the various training areas:

1. The lactate value is fixed for defined loads (= heart rates), so that it is possible to categorise which heart rate belongs to fat metabolism, aerobic or anaerobic carbohydrate metabolism.

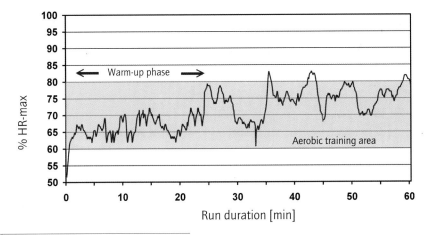

Figure 25: Heart rate (obtained from maximal heart rate) when running with constant loading changes. From the large fluctuations in the heart rate we can see how fast the heart rate reacts to the loading changes. In this example the warm-up phase with a low heart rate values lasts for about 20 minutes. Every individual, but also every group coach can immediately check whether the warm-up speed was correct or too fast.

2. By establishing the maximal heart rate HR_{max}, for which there are currently the following possibilities:

▶ As an objective in the Hollmann formula: $HR_{max} = 220 -$ age (see also Chapter 2.2 "Systole, Diastole, maximal Heart Rate").
▶ In a running test with maximal load (e.g. maximal speed or steep uphill) the highest heart rate will be set as HR_{max}.
▶ Using the S-Series heart rate monitor from Polar, which can measure the maximal heart rate sufficiently accurately at rest.

59

HR_{max} – value = 100% is set for overall comparability. As a rough division:

Heart rate HR < 60% HR_{max} : regenerative fat metabolism

Heart rate HR = 60-80% HR_{max} : partly fat metabolism, partly aerobic carbohydrate metabolism

Heart rate HR > 80% HR_{max} : predominantly to exclusively anaerobic carbohydrate metabolism

The aerobic/anaerobic threshold lies at 75-85% of the maximal heart rate. Below this threshold, i.e. at a loading intensity of HR = 60-80% HR_{max}, lies the optimal endurance training zone with the following positive effects:

- ▶ optimal blood production
- ▶ optimal blood circulation speed
- ▶ maximal oxygen consumption in the capillaries
- ▶ maximal oxygen/CO_2 exchange in the pulmonary alveoli
- ▶ strengthening of the immune system

The correlation between heart rate and load is also dependent on weather conditions, particularly on temperature but also on the runner's state of health. An increase in the heart rate value due to an increase in external temperature is normal. That's why the load in such weather conditions should be reduced. An increased heart rate in normal temperature is, however, a warning signal from the body. Loading reductions are indicated – particularly when the causes have still not been identified. A health check-up is advisable.

Specific training management and monitoring is only possible by measuring the heart rate, to check that training is carried out at the planned loading intensity. It is also appropriate for beginners and fun-runners, as training is often done at too high a loading intensity (> 80%) in the anaerobic zone, and therefore is inefficient.

For very slow runners, particularly overweight ones, the author considers essential the use of a heart rate monitor together with a second stopwatch held by an assistant to eliminate as many overloading risks as possible. Only measuring techniques can counteract the belief that "the more (training) the better". Runners in particular will be surprised at how unusually slow an efficient endurance training session is.

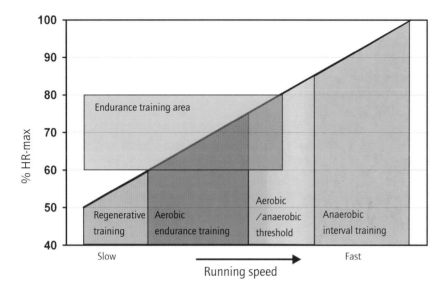

Figure 26: Heart rate values (taken from maximal heart rate) for different training areas.

Heart rate monitors are now available from many manufacturers (Cardiosport, Ciclosport, Phase, Polar). The most accurate are those with a chest sensor and a wristwatch as a receiver. The price range is very high at 50 $ / 30 £ for a simple one and 250 $ / 140 £ for a monitor with PC interface (e.g. Polar S 710 including IR adaptor and analysis software).

The transmitter and receiver batteries last about two years. When you buy them, check out the service address and possibilities for changing batteries, the same is also true for special offers from the discount store. For Polar for example, the transmitter is enclosed and is changed every time you change the batteries in the receiver watch to maintain high accuracy.

For faultless data transmission, there must be enough moisture available between the chest band and the skin. The belt must therefore be dampened with saliva or water. If your skin is very dry, use gel (NACL free).

There can be interference problems when two athletes next to each other are wearing heart rate monitors. Manufacturers try to eliminate this with an automatic modulation of the transmitter frequencies (there are almost no details of this in any supporting documents).

In addition, when buying the equipment, you should check whether the monitor measures the actual heart rate (Polar is as accurate as an ECG) or displays and memorises an average of several pulse beats. Expensive models can be set up with memory interval of e.g. 5, 15, 60 seconds.

There are many kinds of receiver, and they can be divided roughly into four areas of application:

1. Standard watches with heart rate displays as well as adjustable upper and lower limit values. They are intended for runners who know their own training rate zones and train within these limits or specifically want to run at below or above these rates.

2. Watches with message buffers, target areas, average heart rates, etc. for ambitious runners who want to control definite training loads by heart rate.

3. Watches which in addition can measure the resting pulse, the aerobic training area, the proportion of the training in the fat metabolism as well as the calories burnt. The M-Series of POLAR is one of these. Sample comparisons by the author of the lactate level test and the HR_{max} measurement in running tests provide very similar results. The values can be retrieved at will for individual training sessions or added up. These heart rate monitors can really help athletes whose goal is to train in the fat metabolism.
This group also includes models equipped with temperature displays, altimeters or for the collection of data for cyclists.

4. Watches that allow data transfer to PC. Technologically advanced models now have memory capacities of up to 99 hours. The S-Series by POLAR also offers in addition to the functions of the M-Series the measurement of HR_{max} on the basis of individual data, without the need for actually overloading. This enables the risks of maximal loading to be avoided completely.

Such models are an optimal aid for coaches, therapists, training groups or runners who want to know it exactly. Computer analysis can present the chronological heart rate graphically and analyse it (Figure 25). They are ideal for determining the base and monitoring performance, as weekly and monthly overviews are possible. With the aid of diagrams loads can be measured or specifically predetermined and subsequently checked if they have been adhered to, e.g.:

▶ Loading intensity (60, 80, 100%) – training done at the desired level?

▶ Loading rate in the warm-up – are the guidelines for the warm-up phase (Figure 25) followed? One of the most serious mistakes of many solo runners.

▶ Loading reactions to the terrain profile.

▶ Monitoring of loading reductions (pace reduction and the length and location of rest periods) (see also Figures 28, 29).

▶ Changes in the training condition.

▶ Identification of health problems, e.g. raised heart rate during a cold (also not fully cured), mineral deficiencies.

▶ Maintenance of therapeutically prescribed heart rate values in rehabilitation.

One of these is sufficient for a group of runners. Regular heart rate checks can be carried out with just one heart rate monitor.

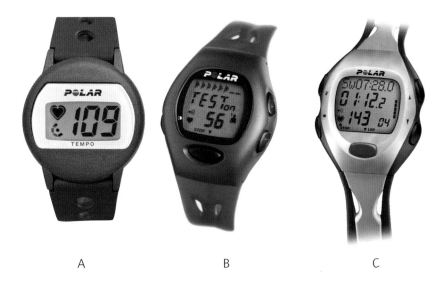

A   B   C

Figure 27: Three examples of POLAR: A: simple model, B: M-Series, C: S-Series.

63

3.2.3   Warming up – the correct Speed

The correct warming-up speed is vital for success both in training and in competition. The warm-up is different from sport to sport and lasts from 30 to 120 minutes. Top marathon runners, e.g. the two-time Olympic champion Waldemar Cierpinski, warm up for one hour; for normal endurance training at least 30 minutes is required. What is the goal and what happens in the body to the transposition and adjustment processes in these 30 minutes?

The cardio-vascular system is constantly aware. It must be informed of every increase in loading. This happens in various ways and has not yet been investigated in detail. Metabolic changes play the leading role in the body along with mental and erotic stimuli.

"Associated innervation" is part of the athlete's mental stimuli, i.e. mental preparation for a specific physical performance. This activates both the cardio-vascular system and the musculature. The exact adjustment to demand of the heart and breathing rate and the blood production of the heart and the depth of breathing are controlled in runners by the increasing build-up of metabolic waste products, particularly lactic acid.

Every increase in pace, be it the transition from walking to running or accelerating when running, like a loading increase when running uphill, represents an increased energy demand for the already working muscles or those brought into action. That is why, as described above, every muscle cell has an immediate energy supply for eight to nine strides. After these few strides, when the oxygen supply has not yet adjusted to the increased demand, the muscle cells shift to anaerobic metabolism and form correspondingly large amounts of lactic acid (lactate).

To enter endurance fat metabolism, the following adjustments must be made in the body:

► Lactate formation in the blood is unavoidable and necessary during the warm-up period. Hence the motto "As much as necessary, as little as possible".
► "As little as possible" can only be reached by running slowly. The heart rate during this period should be less than 70% of the maximum heart rate (cf. Figure 25) and

▶ A drop in oxygen demand should be achieved with short loading reductions. For the beginner this happens with short, maximal t = 15-20 second intervals, for trained runners with a short, deliberate reduction in speed. The emphasis is on short duration, i.e. t = 15-20 seconds. In this length of time, the drop in heart rate (see Figure 21) is still small and the oxygen supply still high. At the same time, though, the oxygen demand is lower due to the reduction in load (see also Figure 21) and the muscle cells are therefore able to form free hydrogen carriers again, thus facilitating the desired aerobic energy metabolism. De Marées calls this the "profitable pause" [48].

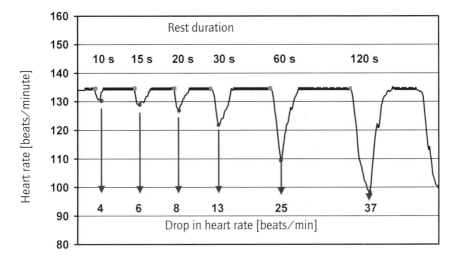

Figure 28: Drop in heart rate (and thus also the oxygen supply) during rest and loading intervals (t = 10-120 seconds). The absolute figure depends on the training condition and the age of the runner.

The rapid drop in heart rate also explains why manual pulse measurements taken by runners from their neck almost never give realistic results.

Extending rest intervals over t = 20 seconds is physiologically unsound. In longer intervals the heart rate and oxygen supply drop too sharply. When loading is resumed, this causes unnecessary anaerobic loading adjustments. Particularly in less well-trained athletes this leads to premature tiredness. Despite this knowledge, you can still see in training manuals, even in the coaching education in some academic colleges, recommended rest durations of t = 1 to 5 minutes.

Likewise, the common practice of interspersing the warm-up period with *five-minutes of stretching exercises*, which after a short warm-up phase is incorporated into an endurance session is at this time physiologically unsound for many reasons. The body and the muscles at that time are not yet warm, only warm muscles should be stretched. If someone absolutely wants to stretch, he should make only short stretches that increase the muscle tone, i.e. the readiness of the muscles to work. All longer-held stretches (see Chapter 5.2 "Flexibility by Stretching and Muscle Strengthening") done at this time lead to a drop in tension in the muscles and diminished performance. Stretching of the musculature that has been shortened by walking and running training is essential to maintain muscle elasticity and joint mobility. It belongs to the warming down phase, i.e. at the end of the training session.

In addition, as demonstrated in Figure 29, the heart rate drops sharply during a stretching pause and at the same time the reduction in muscle activity interrupts the build-up of warmth produced due to increased energy transfer. In the warm-up phase, both disturb the warming-up process and waste training time.

Top marathon runners vary the stretching exercises used during their training sessions between long endurance sessions and speed training. In endurance sessions, stretching takes place at the end of the session. During speed training, however, stretching exercises are carried out after a thorough warm-up phase, with the aim of increasing joint mobility and muscle tone (the tension for working efficiency in the muscles). Stretching exercises for relaxation purposes should also be done at the end of the training session in this case.

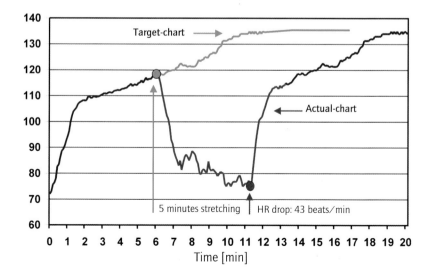

Most runners have experienced the high lactate build up in the leg muscles during the warm-up phase, namely when after 10-20 minutes the legs become "heavy" and you have the feeling: "today it's really not going right". After ten more minutes, the feeling of heaviness suddenly disappears and your legs flow. Now the body is warm, oxygen supply has adjusted to oxygen demand and from now on the energy is produced aerobically.

To be able to supply the working muscles with enough oxygen, the blood stream must be redirected to the muscles with increased oxygen demand. For runners, this means that the capillaries that supply the leg and foot areas must be opened wide, to allow the large increase in blood volume of from about $V = 2$ l/min to $V = 20\text{-}25$ l/min to flow in.

At the same time, the blood supply to the gastro-intestinal tract is cut off. This is why you should not run on a full stomach. Digestion requires a lot of blood. You can either digest or run, not both!

Like a car engine, the complete energy transfer in the muscle and high work rate require an optimal operating temperature. This is $T = 38 - 39°C$ [38]. The muscle temperature in the calf and foot area must be raised by about $= \blacktriangle T\ 10°$ (Figure 30). This is only possible using the warmth built up during energy transfer, not from an external source. That is why we talk about warming up and a warm-up phase.

Likewise, the whole nervous system and coordination control only function optimally at the above-mentioned operating temperature.

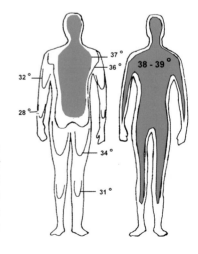

Figure 29 (left page): Stopping to stretch for 5 minutes after a short warm-up phase is physiologically unsound as it causes the heart rate to drop sharply. It disturbs the warm-up process at this point. It belongs at the end of the training session where muscles that have been shortened by the training session are stretched.

Figure 30 (this page): Temperature distribution in the body, left: temperature distribution at rest and at low activity, right: at optimal energy transfer and as a prerequisite for high performance ability, the temperature in the working muscles must be increased to $T = 38\text{-}39°C$. The warming comes from the warmth built up during energy transfer [35].

3.2.4   Consequences for Beginners

Beginners have only small energy reserves available. Their energy should therefore not be "wasted" in anaerobic activity, but treated economically. For this they must run slowly (60-70%) to start with (jogging), which will stimulate the cardio-vascular system and already after a few metres intersperse short breaks of max. t = 20 seconds, in order to make use of the "profitable pause" (Figure 31). In this way even completely untrained beginners can complete a one-hour jog-walk-jog training session without danger of over-exertion [20, 70].

How well this can be put into practice is shown by the heart rate curve of a novice female runner who jogged 5.5 km in one hour with 20 short (about 20 seconds) rests (Figure 32). The rapid drop in heart rate during those intervals shows that short breaks are also effective for little-trained runners.

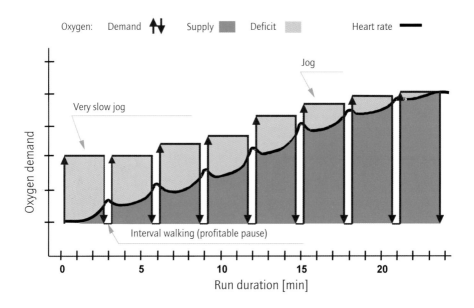

Figure 31: Loading increase in the warm-up phase for the untrained beginner. A slow loading increase brings oxygen supply in line with oxygen demand. For this, the intervals must start very early on and to be beneficial must last only about t = 20 seconds.

The whole secret of success consists of making the breaks (walking intervals) as early on as possible, in any case way before you feel you need one. Figure 33 shows how to situate the "profitable pauses" for a one-hour run for runners of various abilities. On a flat surface, at a running speed of about v = 7-7.5 km/h, a limit area is reached, at which it is possible to jog a whole hour without a break. On an uneven surface, the breaks should take place in the uphill sections, more exactly, in the second half of the uphill section if possible. This is how to reach the optimal balance between working and resting.

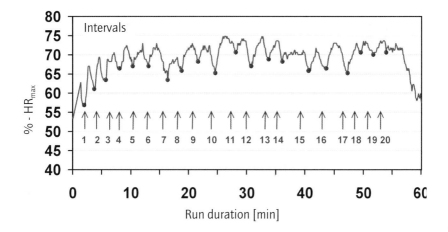

Figure 32: Heart rates (taken from the maximal heart rate) of a participant in a group of beginners from the Darmstadt running club with v = 5.5 km/h. The position of the 20 intervals in this optimally conducted novice group can be clearly recognised. The rapid drop in heart rate during the intervals also shows that the short pauses are effective even for little-trained runners.

If someone running at 8 km/h on a flat surface still needs a rest (breather), they would do better to run a little slower. These rest breaks are required when the runner cannot take any more because he has run too fast. The break is no longer a "profitable pause", but a forced break, for the too high pace has used too much anaerobic energy, and at the same time formed a lot of lactic acid. Running more slowly and/or taking earlier rest breaks can avoid this.

69

For novice runners it is very difficult, if not impossible, to find their own optimal speed without guidance. At school they have only learnt that they have to run fast. They think they should still do this and run off until they are exhausted and think that this sport is not for them. This is when a qualified coach is needed, and a heart rate monitor.

Running speed [km/h]
Rest breaks

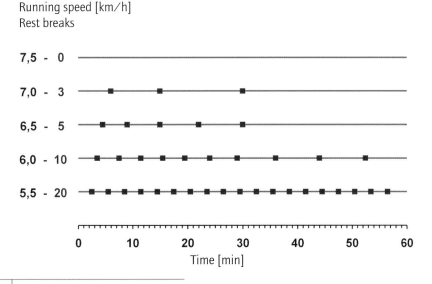

Figure 33: Running (and jogging) and rest sequences for beginners and little-trained runners for a training session of t = 60 minutes. The early breaks are called "profitable pauses" and are a decisive factor in the success of the training session.

3.2.4.1 Stitch

A stitch is mainly a beginners' problem. Its exact cause is not yet known. There are three current theories:

1. An over-full stomach filled with insufficiently digested food, which provokes stomach aches on the left side of the body.

2. Capsule tension in the spleen and/or liver due to the high reverse blood flow from the leg-hip area, which causes pain on the right side.

3. Insufficient oxygen supply to the diaphragm. This causes pain on the right and left sides.

Different kinds of stitch (see below) can be classified according to when they appear:

▶ The first kind of stitch appears just after the start of the run, after about 5-15 minutes. Its suspected cause is a momentarily too high blood circulation in the body or an under-supply of oxygen to the diaphragm muscles. This kind of stitch occurs mainly in the first week of training – a well-trained runner rarely experiences it.

This can be counteracted by slowing down (reduction of oxygen demand) or, and in most cases this works, by deliberate breathing (exhaling). The stitch disappears after a few minutes. It disappears in any case after 20-25 minutes when the body is warmed up and the oxygen demand is reduced.

▶ The second kind – usually appearing after about 40 minutes or more – is mainly due to digestive problems, e.g. flatulence in the intestine. It affects runners, especially females, with slow digestion, who have overeaten all day or women who have eaten food that is too stodgy.

Running stimulates intestinal activity in which intestinal gases can be formed. To get rid of them as soon as possible, strong stomach massage helps some people, for others, only a quick jump in the bushes works. Regular running improves digestion so that after a short while this problem disappears. Also, those who have relied on medicinal digestive aids will soon be able to dispense with them.

This kind of stitch can be avoided by not eating too heavily before running and by emptying the bowels as regularly as possible.

▶ The third kind is normally only experienced by competitive runners, e.g. elite athletes, when they have a problem with the speed of the race, or by fun-runners in the marathon, when they hit "the wall" after three or four hours. In this phase the pulse increases without an increase in load (exhaustion pulse), the energy reserves are empty and the muscles are largely in hyperlactatemia.

This can only be prevented by correct pace distribution during the race, and counteracted only by drastic pace reduction.

3.2.5   Consequences for trained Athletes

The mechanisms of correct warming up apply to everyone, even trained runners. It does not matter if someone is doing a training run or a long timed distance. It can be a 2,000 m or 3,000 m for a sports award or a 15 or 30 minute running badge at the running club.

71

Even for these goals, it is still necessary to warm up by slowly increasing the pace for at least 30 minutes. Good performances are only possible after an adequate warm-up.

The often-expressed fear: "but then I'll be exhausted already" is unfounded, if the load is increased slowly and early "profitable pauses" are incorporated in the form of walking breaks or speed reductions.

Another example (Figure 34) shows what happens when two runners with different training backgrounds run for one hour on hilly terrain and the little-trained athlete (A) tries to keep up with the trained athlete (B).

The high lactate value (5.6 mmol/l) of runner A and especially the increase in heart rate difference compared to runner B shows that runner A has done an exhausting anaerobic interval training session instead of endurance training in fat metabolism. Runner B, on the other hand, has carried out an optimal endurance training session.

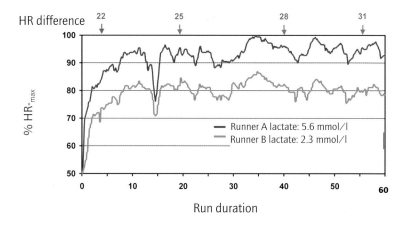

Figure 34: The heart rate curve shows what happens when two runners with different training states train together and the better runner sets the pace. For B (lower curve) it was an optimal training run with a lactate value of 2.3 mmol/l, for A is an exhausting anaerobic inverval training session in the anaerobic area with a lactate value of 5.6 mmol/l. In addition it shows the increasing hyperlacatemia and fatigue of A. In the training session, the pulse difference of A compared to B rises from 22 to 31 pulse beats.

3.2.5.1 Tips for Marathon Running

To tackle the marathon distance of 42.195 km (26.2 miles) is an irresistible challenge for many trained runners. For the first time, it is a matter of just "arriving, no matter in what time." The second time, time is an issue.

The marathon is the hardest long distance race, as for optimal performance it must be run predominantly in the fat metabolism with loading peaks in the aerobic carbohydrate metabolism. This demand is the crucial point, as only heart rate measurement can tell him which metabolic area he is running in. This does not only concern fun runners; at elite level it can make the difference between winning and losing.

To run a marathon in optimal time is therefore a question of head over heart [40, 52, 53, 72]. After a specific warm-up, the time guidelines for the first 10 km must be adhered to strictly. The runner may not let himself be swept along euphorically at the pace of better runners. The sooner he reaches the fat metabolism area and sticks to it, the better his finishing time will be. A high proportion of anaerobic activity in the first 10 km means that the runner will hit "the wall" at around 35 km.

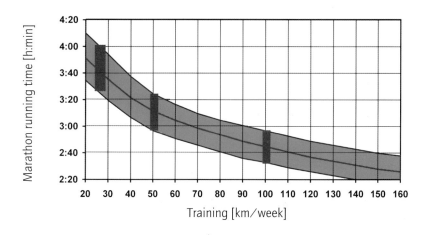

Figure 35: Marathon running times against an optimally performed training session for elite and grass roots runners [52].

Another mental aid is not to think of the whole 42 km length, but to break it down into smaller sections. The easiest is by kilometre. From the first kilometre, the runner always thinks only about managing the kilometre he is running at the time. This produces a feeling of success after each successfully completed kilometre. This gives some structure and prevents the crippling and destructive fear of not being able to manage the whole distance.

In race preparation, over-ambitious fun runners, particularly those who train alone, can be seen training too intensively, both in terms of training volume and running speed [45].

Neumann [52] has carried out a survey on training volume with 40-55 year-old runners (see Figure 35). The relatively low training volumes shown will surprise many runners. They are realistic. They require a targeted training in the aerobic area (HR_{max} = 60-80%), good coordination and elastic muscles. The eliminated running sessions must be replaced with muscle stretching and strengthening sessions (see Chapter 5.2 "Flexibility by Stretching and Muscle Strengthening") and Coordination training (see Chapter 5.1: "Coordination Training for Running Style").

As far as running speed is concerned, fun runners and competitive runners should follow the example of successful world-class runners, who run the marathon distance at 20 km/hour, train for endurance at about 15 km/hour (= 75%) and run regenerative sessions at about 10-12 km/hour (= 50%). It is easier to reproduce this using a heart rate monitor than by feeling alone!

The lowest training speed in the aerobic area for a marathon runner should be v = 10 km/hour. This gives a final finishing time of 4 to 4:30 hours. According to the author's experience, this goal can be achieved on an average of 35 km/week, including one weekly 20 km session and a 30 km session eight and four weeks before the marathon.

3.2.6 Training Camps

Elite athletes regularly take part in training camps. They are an integral part of training plans, details of which are organised according to training condition and training goal.

Lower-level runners, however, very often see training camps as the possibility of ironing out their training deficits. They approach their training intensively as a result. They often train several times a day, e.g. a gentle run in the morning, speed training before lunch, a long run after lunch and stretching in the evening. The range of performance is greater than in the training group at home and the best set a pace that most of the weaker runners want to keep up with.

A training volume and intensity that double or even triple overnight will achieve nothing positive. Such jumps in loading drastically reduce the possibility of regeneration between sessions. Many athletes return from training camps completely worn out and need long regeneration periods in which to regain fitness. There are rarely any discernable training effects. Athletes who have to keep an eye on their immune system are advised not attend training camps.

3.2.7 Running with Children

Van Aaaken has shown that children and youngsters can easily run long distances. Damage to health is hitherto unknown. Children can start running at five or six years old, and prefer to run with their parents to running in special children's groups. They need a lot of vocal encouragement though, and someone to chat to when they are running. Training together can have a positive effect on the relationship between parents and children. It requires a partnership, in which running for fun takes precedence over pressure to train and achieve results. If vocal encouragement is lacking, though they will get bored and give up.

Children and young people of normal weight have the great advantage of being light, combined with a strength/efficiency ratio that is normally better than that of adults. There is no real uniform standard of running speed, but children aged between five and ten can, depending on their age, run at about 5 – 10 km/hour after a few days' training.

You cannot push children too hard over long distances. **If they can't go on they just stop (without warning!).** This is a problem for parents and coaches. The children just can't go on! Many adults can't accept this, and instead encourage or force their children to carry on running they take the fun out of it. These parents should take to heart: "Forget pressure, only if your children enjoy running will they get results."

The middle-distance events, over 400-1,500 m, are very problematic for children though. Due to their low body mass, their lactate tolerance is a lot lower than that of adults [6, 4]. These distances are hard for this age group, as they must be run exclusively in anaerobic metabolism, and should only be tackled after a thorough warm-up. In many races, particularly in fun runs, warm-ups are deplorable. The author has too often seen crying children on the track and screeching parents and coaches on the sidelines.

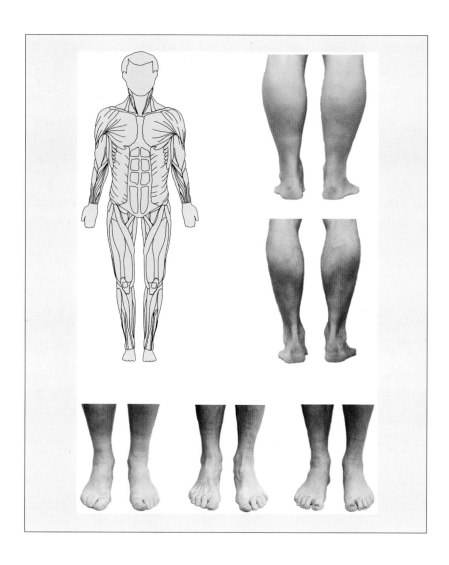

4   Biomechanical Aspects of Running

"Walking is better for the joints than running", it says in all the walking guides. But is this generalisation always true? The answer is a definite "NO", as joint loading depends on muscle elasticity. This can be illustrated by an example. If a maximal walking speed of v = 8 km/h is reached because the walker's leg muscles do not allow a higher speed, their elasticity is also exhausted at this speed. If the same person can also run at v = 10-11 km/h, then his joint loading at a running speed of v = 8 km/h, the same speed at which he was walking, is lower than when walking, as his muscles absorb the shock with optimal elasticity.

These questions can only be answered for individuals, not as generalisations. This also demonstrates the observation that there are athletes who can now only walk due to joint damage, others have joint pain when they walk but are able to carry on running.

4.1   Bones and Ligaments

The human skeleton consists of about 220 bones of various shape and type. They are kept in place by millions of smaller (see Figure 36) and larger (see Figure 37) ligaments. The ligaments also stabilise the joints and limit their mobility and keep the long tendons in place (see Figure 52).

Broken bones are rare in running. As for the ligaments, consisting of very compact, rigid, poorly vascularised tissue, it is almost only the lower retaining ligament of the calf muscle and the tendons (see Figure 44) that are ever damaged by overstretching when spraining an ankle. There are three degrees of injury: partial tear, complete tear and bone tear. Today these injuries are no longer operated on as they were in the past, but taped up, and rested with vacuum splints or special splint boots covering just the injured area.

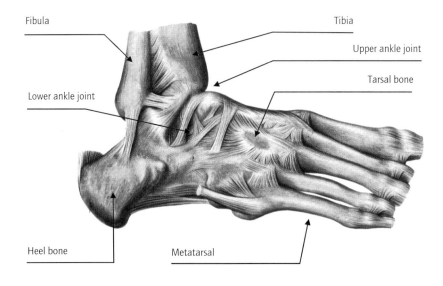

Fibula

Tibia

Upper ankle joint

Tarsal bone

Lower ankle joint

Heel bone

Metatarsal

Figure 36: Ligaments of the ankle [78].

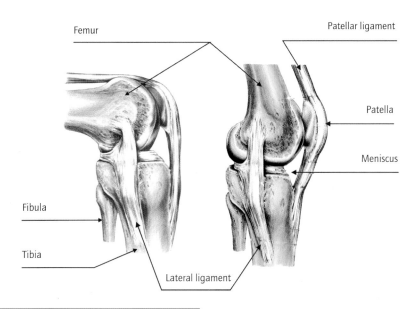

Femur

Patellar ligament

Patella

Meniscus

Fibula

Tibia

Lateral ligament

Figure 37: Patellar and lateral ligaments of the bent (left) and straight (right) knee joint [78].

4.2   Muscles and Tendons

Muscles and tendons always form a unit, as every muscle has a tendon at each end to connect it to the bone to which is it attached. This gives rise to a kinetic (movement) chain [4]: *bone-tendon-muscle-tendon-bone* (see Figure 38). Muscle contraction moves the bones, to which the tendons are attached, over one or more joints (as pivots).

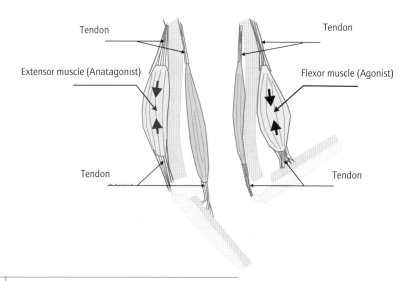

Figure 38: Kinetic movement chain: bone-tendon-muscle-tendon-bone. The extensor and flexor muscle-pair (antagonist and agonist) must be trained equally [67].

The muscle can only work in one direction: "It can only actively contract as a flexor (agonist)". Which is why every muscle needs an opponent, a stretcher (antagonist) that stretches out the contacted muscle again (see Figure 38). This muscle-pair must be balanced. One-sided training, where only one muscle is strengthened, gives rise to muscular imbalances, which has serious health consequences. The vast majority of all back pain culminating in slipped disks is due to such imbalances!

Runners in particular must watch out for this imbalance, for as the muscle chain in Figure 39 [75] shows, they only train the plantar, calf, quadriceps and gluteus maximus muscles. These muscles are strengthened in every training session and are continually being shortened. Only regular stretching can counteract this and maintain full muscle elasticity.

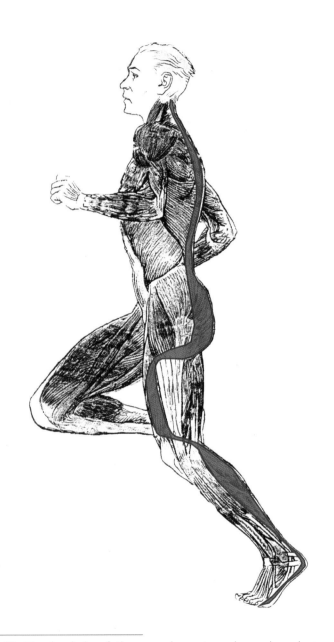

Figure 39: Muscle chain of the runner's most used muscles: plantar, calf, quadriceps and gluteus maximus muscles.

The extensors of the back muscles are the long and oblique abdominal muscles (Figure 40). They are not trained by walking or running, so this must be done in separate training sessions (stretching and strengthening exercises). If the abdominal muscles are neglected and become too weak, the back muscles are shortened and the back becomes hollow [46] (Figure 41). The increased curvature reduces the mobility of the spine and pressure caused by the one-sided loading of the vertebrae causes back pain. The hips also tilt forwards, reducing the lifting angle of the thighs, i.e. the runner's stride will be shorter and he will run more slowly.

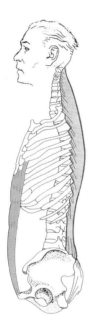

Stomach and back muscles

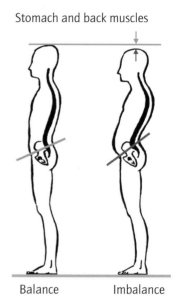

Balance   Imbalance

Figure 40 (left): Abdominal and back muscles must balance each other. Imbalances are the main cause of all back pain culminating in slipped disk. Walking and running do not train the abdominal muscles; they must be strengthened in separate training sessions.

Figure 41 (right): One-sided training of the back muscles leads to hollowing of the back with a one-sided loading of the vertebrae. The hips tilt forwards, thus reducing the lifting angle of the thighs and the runner's stride length.

Another commonly seen imbalance in runners is that between the adductors and abductors. If the adductors are too weak, it makes the legs and feet turn outwards (Figure 42). Such runners are called "10 to 2 runners" due to their foot placement (Figure 43). These imbalances have three disadvantages for those affected: The knee joint is unequally loaded, the stride length can be reduced by up to two centimetres due to the outward turn of the feet and the toe-off power is reduced by the outwards-turned part. This wastes time and strength in a race. Only specific strength training of the adductors with gymnastic exercises or on the relevant equipment in the weights room or gym can eliminate this imbalance.

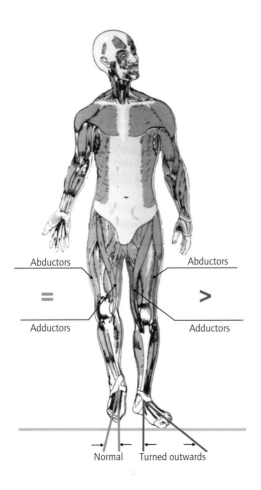

Figure 42: Left: correct foot placement – abductors and adductors are balanced. Right: outwards turned foot placement – imbalance between abductors and adductors leading to unequal loading of the knee joint.

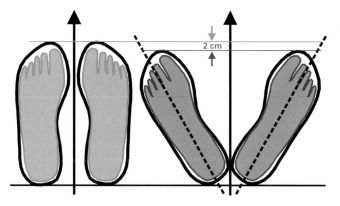

Figure 43: Right: incorrect foot position about 30° out reduces the stride length by about 2 cm and also reduces the toe-off power in the direction of movement.

The stride length can be lengthened if the runner straightens his whole leg by deliberately tensing the hamstring muscles (Figure 44), thereby lifting his body. This also requires additional strength training, e.g. deliberately straightening and tensing on each stride, as this muscle area is otherwise hardly trained by running alone.

Just how important the regular stretching of the trained muscles is, is also shown by the research of Jeschke/Hietkamp [41], Neumann [54] and Wolpert [79], who have also noted greater susceptibility to injury of stiffer runners along with a decrease in muscle elasticity due to shortening.

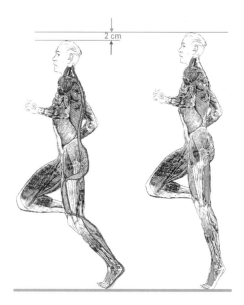

Figure 44: Deliberate tensing of the hamstring muscles (right) straightens the leg and lengthens the stride.

4.2.1 Muscle Action: Heel and Toe Running

Whether runners make ground contact with the ball of the foot or the heel depends on running speed. Sprinters and middle-distance runners run on the balls of the foot. About 95% of long distance runners are heel runners. There is also a transition area covering very slow novice runners and older runners, who touch down with the whole foot.

The muscle action in the touch-down phase is very different in the two running styles. In Figure 45 the three large muscle groups of the lower leg are highlighted.

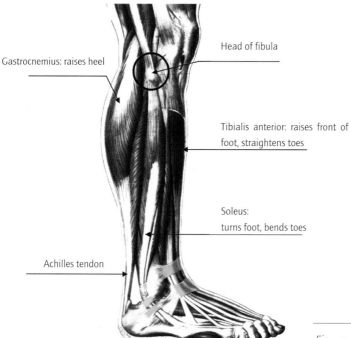

Gastrocnemius: raises heel

Head of fibula

Tibialis anterior: raises front of foot, straightens toes

Soleus: turns foot, bends toes

Achilles tendon

Figure 45: Selected muscle groups of the lower leg [46]

The front foot runner touches down with the ball of the foot and toes. To do this he extends the foot using the gastrocnemius muscle. The knee is slightly bent at the same time, so that the foot strike impact can be absorbed by muscle elasticity.

In the second phase, in a few milliseconds the heel swings at very high speed towards the ground, usually without touching it. The rapid swing of the heel to the ground also stretches the calf muscles at the same speed, causing a very high tensile loading on the Achilles tendon.

This high tensile loading frequently leads to overloading, particularly when the calf muscles are shortened due to lack of stretching, causing inflammation of the Achilles tendon or tears in the sheath surrounding it (see Figure 53), which can very soon become chronic. Such Achilles tendon problems are almost exclusively seen in long distance runners who have moved up from short or middle distance and maintained their front-foot running style.

One possible remedy is to change to running on the heel. A pre-requisite for such a change is a change in the movement sequence (see Chapter 5.1 "Coordination Training for Running Style"), which not all runners find possible.

Out of ignorance, novice runners almost always try to run on the front of the foot in their first training session. Trainers or coaches should ensure the transfer the running style to the back foot, which is easy at this stage. As they are not used to running on the front of the foot, after a few metres novice runners get overloading and cramping in the gastrocnemius and soleus muscles.

Beginners can initially get soreness in the head of the gastrocnemius muscle. The tendons of many muscle groups are concentrated in this area, and they are suddenly activated by unfamiliar training. Such soreness normally disappears after 4-6 weeks without further treatment. If it lasts longer, a sports physician should be consulted.

The heel runner's gastrocnemius muscles in the phase are largely relaxed on heel strike. The soleus muscle is mainly responsible for the stabilisation of the leg. For more on rolling characteristics, see Chapter 9.1.2.5 "Heel Strike, Mid-stance and Toe-off phases".

Walkers always touch down with the heel. The tibialis muscles (Figure 45) play a much more important role for walkers than runners, as their "foot lifting" function is much more important. If a runner walks at unaccustomed high speed and/or with badly laced shoes (bad foot control), he notices overloading in the tibialis area.

4.2.2 Muscle Structure and Function

Details of muscle structure and function are described very thoroughly in the literature [48, 49], so in this book I will only give the details that are necessary to understand what happens in the body during endurance training.

Figure 46 shows the structure of a muscle, in this case the biceps muscle, a typical skeletal muscle. Every muscle consists of a **muscle bundle**, which is composed of **muscle fibres**. The muscle fibre is also a muscle cell, which has access to several cell nuclei (dark red bodies in Figure 46) whose origin is not yet clear. Muscle fibres are extremely thin. Their diameter is on average 20 μm = 0.02 mm, similar to human hair. They can be up to 15 cm long.

A single muscle fibre is, as shown in Figure 46, again a bundle of about 1 μm (0.001mm) thin **myofibrils**. These myofibrils are partitioned into **sarcomeres**, single, very short sections, the real operations area of the muscle.

The "partitions" of these sections are called **Z disks**, as on both sides they have thin "arms" (**actin filaments**) with a Z-shaped structure. In between there are **myosin filaments** with about 150 contact fingers.

A working area is activated by a **motor nerve impulse** (motor function = the movement of controlling nerve impulses) on a **myoceptor** (Figure 47). The number of sarcomere units controlled by one myoceptor is very different from muscle to muscle. The smaller the number, the more precisely movement can be controlled, e.g. in the hand or eye areas. In the buttocks and thighs, however, very large areas of muscle of controlled by a small number of myoceptors.

Figure 46: (right side): Muscle formation: muscle bundle, muscle fibre, myofibril, sarcomere, Z disk, actin filament, myosin filament.

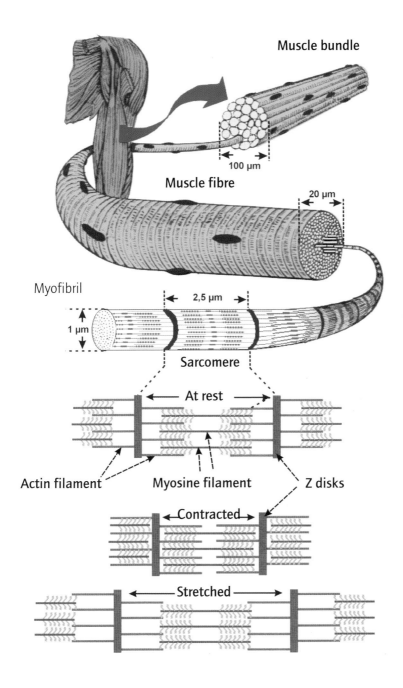

Muscle bundle

100 µm

Muscle fibre

20 µm

Myofibril

2,5 µm

1 µm

Sarcomere

At rest

Actin filament   Myosine filament   Z disks

Contracted

Stretched

Another factor affecting control is that the myoceptors react with differing voltage intensities (20-50 mV). They obey the so-called "all or nothing" law, i.e. if the voltage is sufficient, they are activated, if not, nothing happens (see Chapter 4.5 "Control of Muscle Activites by the Brain and nervous System").

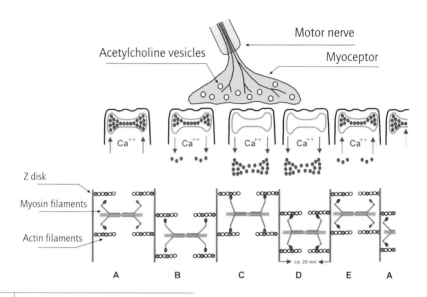

Figure 47: Diagram of the activation of a muscle fibre stimulation of a myoceptor by a motor nerve, triggering a multiple-stage chemical-electrical process, in which, among other things, calcium is released in the sarcomere for the activation process. A: rest; B: start of the stimulation with calcium. Release and tensing of the myosin heads; C: electrical connection between the myosin heads and the actin filaments; D: contraction (2 x about 10 nm) by release of the energy stored in the tensed myosin heads; E: depolarisation with reverse flow of the calcium into the vesicles; A: rest.

At complete activation (C), there is an electrical coupling between the myosin heads and the actin fibres. The muscle can now remain in this state (C), i.e. the myosin finger "only" couples with the actin, there is no other activity. Then the muscle is tensed and can receive the forces working on it. The author calls this state "passive" (see Chapter 4.2.4 "Active and passive Muscle Loading").

However, if the myosin fingers release manufactured kinetic energy as they tense up, they move the coupled actin arms about 20 nm (10 nm on each side) into the centre (D). This telescope-like push can be repeated until the sarcomere has shortened by about 30% (contraction). This triggers a movement of the body (walking, running, lifting, etc.) The author calls this state "active".

In both cases, the coupling lasts for as long as the electrical tension exists. As soon as it declines, the calcium returns back to its vesicles and the electrical connection is broken. The filaments can then either be re-activated or slide over each other, i.e. be stretched.

The number of activated work units (sarcomeres) within a myofibril determines the efficiency of the muscle, i.e. how much power it can absorb and produce. The number of activated work units is increased up to a force component of 50%, then the impulse frequency is increased, up to 1000 impulses per second.

4.2.3   Red and white Muscle Fibres

Red muscle fibres contain more of the red pigment, myoglobin, which stores oxygen inside the muscle cell (like haemoglobin in the blood that transports oxygen). The red fibres work at relatively low impulse frequencies and are hence known as "slow twitch" fibres. In combination with the greater oxygen supply from the augmented myoglobin, they also result in endurance musculature.

White muscle fibres react particularly to high impulse frequencies and are therefore called "fast twitch" fibres and are used for very short-term effort by strength musculature. There is also a third kind of fibre that occupies a middle ground between the two.

The proportion of white (fast-twitch) and red (slow-twitch) muscle fibres is genetically pre-determined and is influenced by movement behaviour in childhood and adolescence. Endurance training can convert red fibres to white to a limited extent. Until now, it was thought that white fibres could not be converted to red. This assumption is currently being challenged by basic research. It is suspected that so-called neutral fibres can be converted to red or white, depending on demand.

4.2.4   Active and passive Muscle Loading

Active Loading

Active means the voluntary tension of a muscle to hold an object or to carry out a movement, e.g. climbing stairs, running uphill, sprinting, jumping, lifting, etc. The activation of the necessary work units is normally automatic and involuntary for as long as the strength, e.g. to climb a step lasts.

The limiting factor in active loading is the adequate oxygen supply of the muscles over the working period. If the oxygen supply can no longer meet the demand, energy production in the working muscles changes from aerobic to anaerobic, a bye-product of which is lactic acid (Chapter 3.1 "Obtaining Energy from Carbohydrates and Fats"). This acidifies and hyperlactates the blood until total exhaustion is reached.

Passive Loading

In passive loading, the muscle must absorb external loads and forces working on it. Some examples are: the bodyweight when getting off a chair, walking and running downhill, or the weight when catching a heavy object, etc. For this the body must adjust itself to the anticipated load and pre-tense the relevant muscle mass. But how does the body know how much muscle mass to pre-tense? It doesn't, but learns by experience. For example, an experienced mountain guide doesn't get aching muscles even after walking up a steep hill for hours; the inexperienced novice can't avoid it.

Aching muscles almost always occur, even in trained athletes, when they carry out new movements for the first time, even if it just unaccustomed bending over to pick strawberries.

4.2.5   Muscle Soreness

The most common answer to the question "What is muscle soreness?" is still "The accumulation of lactic acid". This answer is wrong – it has not only been suspected for a long time, but also known since 1988 [10] and now corroborated again [11]. Lactic acid is formed by very intensive **"active"** muscle loading: aching muscles occur after **"passive"** mechanical muscle loading. How does this overloading happen? It depends on the body's previous experience with the anticipated load. If it has sufficient experience, e.g. the mountain guide, then the necessary number of work units will be activated to deal with the forces working on the muscle. In the absence of this experience, the number will be activated by guesswork, which is very hard to judge visually. If the task looks difficult, normally sufficient numbers are activated. If it looks easy, e.g. getting off a chair or walking or running downhill, then too few work units are activated to handle the forces acting on the body. As the body weight is predetermined, there is inevitably local mechanical overloading in the sarcomeres. The electrical coupling between the myosin heads and the actin fibres is more stable than the strength of the Z disks, which tear. This can be proven with electron-microscope photographs (Figure 48).

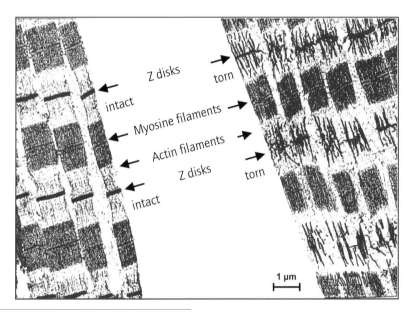

Figure 48: Electron-microscope photograph of myofibrils. Left: intact Z disks; right: torn Z disks.

This tearing does not cause pain, as there are no pain receptors inside the fibres. The performance ability of the muscle is immediately impaired, though. The pain – muscle soreness – is only felt after a few hours, when the break-down products reach the surface of the muscle, and the well-known protection blocking and pain reactions are triggered.

Compared to the tearing of muscle fibres, the tearing of Z disks is actually quite positive. The scars formed after muscle fibres are torn are not observed after the tearing of Z disks. The sarcomere areas concerned break down completely. It is even suspected that in these areas there are more myofibrils available than before, so that the muscle can be strengthened. Such a myofibril increase is also considered to be a positive effect of strength training on the strengthening of the muscles.

Intra-muscular coordination improves very rapidly, so that muscle soreness is typical for the starting phase of sporting activity and the practising of a new movement. It cannot be prevented, but thorough warming up and a slow increase in loading can help.

Muscle soreness is a mechanical injury [10, 11, 24]. That is why, contrary to earlier theories, the muscle area concerned should not be massaged or intensively loaded. Light exercise, e.g. cycling, and anything that encourages blood circulation, e.g. hot baths or saunas, is recommended.

Symptoms similar to those of muscle soreness occur after very long-lasting loads, e.g. the marathon, when the metabolic processes in the muscle are impaired due to insufficient energy and electrolyte supply. In this case, too, overloading occurs when the bodyweight is absorbed as a "passive" load in the heel-strike phase [10, 11].

4.2.6   Muscle Cramps, Tension, Pulls and Tears

Muscle cramps and tension are not injuries; the muscle is just under electrical tension [50, 74]. The electrical connection between myosin heads and actin filaments (see Figure 47, parts C and D) can not be broken, as the sensitive electrolyte equilibrium (of, among others, magnesium, calcium, potassium, sodium), is upset due to e.g. long-lasting demand or, in particular, to heat.

When a muscle is pulled, the fine sheath surrounding the muscle (muscle fascia) is injured. It happens when the muscle is stretched more than 170%. Complete muscle pulls are very rare. Excessive passive muscle loading normally gives rise to muscle fibre tears or tears of one or more muscle fibres.

4.3   Joints

The ankle, knee and hip joints in particular are loaded when running. The joint surfaces at the ends of bones are specially developed. They consist of a layer of cartilage whose outer edge is bathed in synovial fluid (Figure 49). The entire joint is enclosed in a joint lining and the joint capsule.

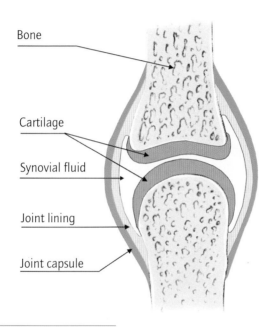

Bone

Cartilage

Synovial fluid

Joint lining

Joint capsule

Figure 49: Diagram of a joint [46].

Despite the great importance of the cartilage for movement, after the age of 20 its supply with nutrients is very poor, since at this age, the direct arterial supply is cut. From then on it is supplied is by "kneading in" the synovial fluid into the cartilage, i.e. joint mobility is a prerequisite for joint nutrition.

The surface of the cartilage appears to be completely smooth, however, electron-microscope magnification (Figure 50) shows that it is scaly and, like human hair, is subject to constant wear and tear. Underneath, collagen tissue covers the hollows of the cartilage cells [24]. The collagen tissue consists of thin protein threads that are arranged to form an elastic dividing layer which can absorb or reduce shock to the joint.

Cartilage surface

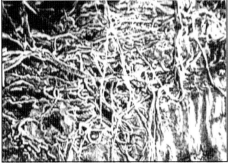

Underneath:
Elastic, collagen dividing tissue

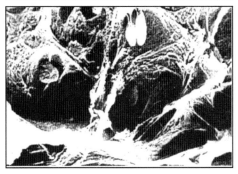

Underneath:
Cartilage threads
Cartilage cells

Figure 50: Electron microscope photographs. Top: cartilage surface. Centre: collagen dividing tissue. Bottom: cartilage threads and cartilage cells.

High-pressure loading or very long-lasting loads, e.g. marathon running, cause great wear and tear of the cartilage surface. After such loads, sufficient regeneration must be allowed. The problem is that no-one knows exactly how long is required for complete regeneration. It is suspected that the time required is a multiple of the cardio-vascular and energy regeneration.

Regeneration does not mean rest! On the contrary, light exercise, e.g. light cycling and especially water jogging, encourage the supply to and thus the regeneration of the cartilage.

Incorrect loading by pointed instead of completely flat loading of the cartilage due to congenital incorrect posture or acquired postural defects, e.g. hollow back (see Figure 41) or leg turn out (see Figures 42, 43), in the long-term always lead to increased wear and tear of the cartilage surface. Incorrect loading due to too soft and inadequate shoe support is particularly frequent (Figure 51) (see Chapter 9 "Shoes"). If the surface is injured in this way, arthritis is almost unavoidable, as there is as yet no proven way to repair defective cartilage. Acquired postural defects and the related incorrect loading can be reduced or even avoided by specific compensation and strengthening exercises!

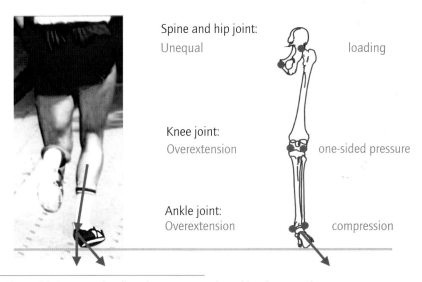

Spine and hip joint:
Unequal   loading

Knee joint:
Overextension   one-sided pressure

Ankle joint:
Overextension   compression

Figure 51: Incorrect loading due to too weak and inadequate shoe support.

Joints that come under particular stress have an additional cartilage to improve shock absorption in the joint. In the spine there are inter-vertebral disks, in the knee the inner and outer meniscus (Figure 52). Despite these two menisci, the knee is the joint most susceptible to incorrect loading. The causes of incorrect loading can often be found in the "shoe + foot" combination (see Figures 63, 64, 66, 69). **If these are not corrected, then all medical treatment of the knee will be unsuccessful in the long run.**

To sum up, it may be said that joint wear and tear is caused by both walking and running. Man has been a "walking animal" for millions of years. We know that walkers and runners were not immune from joint wear and tear, based on the existence of congenital postural defects, and especially the variety of postural defects and shock injuries. If you look at Figure 52: in the vast majority of cases, cruciate ligament injuries occur in the front ligament. If its function is not restored, particularly after a tear, there will be lifelong instability in the joint especially when walking or running on uneven ground.

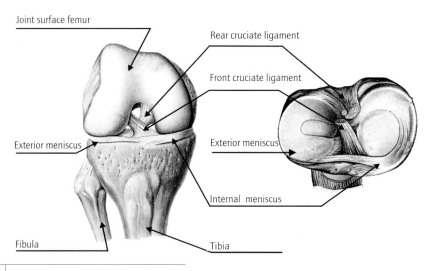

Figure 52: Knee joint with inner and outer meniscus, front and rear cruciate ligaments [78].

4.4   Tendon Sheathes

Tendon sheathes act as "guide tubes" for the tendons, to allow them to slide easily over bones and joints. They can be several centimetres long (Figure 53).

The Achilles tendon sheath is many front-of-foot runners' greatest weak spot. Chapter 4.2.1 "Muscle Action: Heel and Toe Running" explains how it can be exonerated.

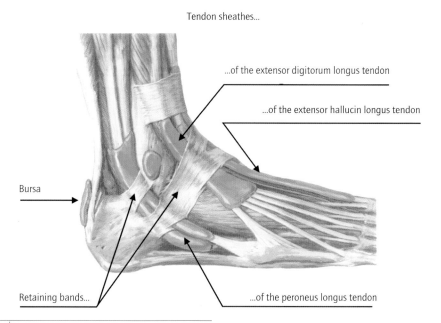

Tendon sheathes...

...of the extensor digitorum longus tendon

...of the extensor hallucin longus tendon

Bursa

Retaining bands...

...of the peroneus longus tendon

Figure 53: Tendon sheathes of various muscle functions. The weak point of many front-of-foot runners is the tendon sheath of the Achilles tendon.

4.5 Control of Muscle Activities by the Brain and nervous System

The cerebrum (see Figure 54) acts as a motivation centre, in which the decisions for an action, i.e. conscious seeing, hearing, speaking, moving, etc are taken by "active" thinking processes [37,74]. The movement area, for the activation of the skeletal musculature, is called the motor zone, and is divided into three parts in the cerebrum according to the movement possibilities of the separate parts of the body, the head, hand and torso and leg muscles.

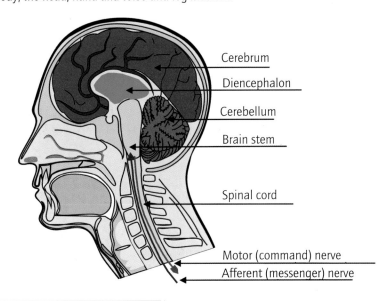

Cerebrum

Diencephalon

Cerebellum

Brain stem

Spinal cord

Motor (command) nerve

Afferent (messenger) nerve

Figure 54: The principal movement control areas of the brain.

The transfer of a decision from a planned movement to an executed movement takes place over several strides and a simplified example of running is shown below:

1. In the motor zone of the cerebrum: decision of the athlete to run. This "command" continues to the diancephalon.
2. In the diancephalon, the *programme store* of the brain: enquiry in the *programme library* as to whether there is a suitable *movement pattern* for running already available. If there is a suitable or roughly suitable programme available, it is forwarded to the cerebellum. If nothing suitable is found, the movement cannot be performed. It must first be learnt in detail or as a whole. This is also the case when movement patterns are destroyed by accidents.

3. In the cerebellum: establishing of the chronological sequence of the separate programme stages. So, a step must be broken down into successive chronological stages: transfer of bodyweight onto the left leg as support leg – raising and forwards movement of the relieved right leg – pressure force in the left leg builds up – left leg straightens and unwind process begins to pre-tense the muscles of the right leg, ready be able to absorb the bodyweight during the foot-strike phase, etc. This programme concept then continues to the brain stem.

4. In the brain stem: In this coordination centre, there is constant coordination of the separate programme steps with information from the sensory organs (eyes e.g. about uneven terrain, obstacles; ears, e.g. about traffic noises; skin, e.g. about temperature, wind, etc.) as well as feedback from the body about the tenseness of the muscles and the joint positions. At the same time, control of the posture and support motor ability intervenes, i.e. the involuntary muscular activity that stabilises the body and maintains its equilibrium. The command impulses now ready are transferred to the motor nerve tracts in the spinal chord.

5. In the spinal chord:
continuation of the command impulse in the motor nerve tracts down to the relevant section of the spine (Figure 55). There the impulses are transferred to the "corridors", to the anterior horn.

6. In the anterior horn: the anterior horn cells are corridors, as they are not only the place where motor command impulses are sent from the brain to muscle cells, but also where all afferent signals come together, received from the receptors (reception sensors) of the internal organs,

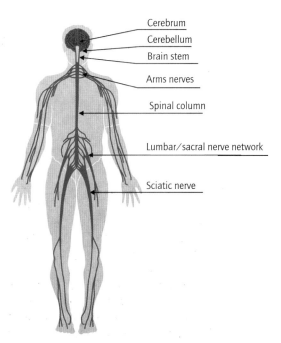

Cerebrum
Cerebellum
Brain stem
Arms nerves
Spinal column
Lumbar/sacral nerve network
Sciatic nerve

Figure 55: The spinal column consists, from top to bottom, of seven cervical, twelve thoracic, five lumbar and three sacral vertebrae. The arm nerves originate from the lower cervical vertebrae. The starting point of the bottom and leg nerves, including the sciatic nerve, is situated in the lumbar vertebrae.

the body surface, for the tenseness of the muscles, the position of the joints, etc., and sent back to the brain. In these corridors, direct bridge circuits are possible between the motor and afferent nerves, in order to shorten the long pathways to the brain and back, when parts of the body must be moved away from danger zones via lightning fast reflexes.

From the anterior horn the command impulses of the brain are sent on down motor nerves to the motor end plates (see Figure 47).

7. In the motor endplate: the incoming electrical command impulses trigger a chemical reaction which leads to the activation of the appropriate muscle area (see Figure 47).

There is constant feedback between the separate brain areas (cerebrum, diancephalon, cerebellum and brain stem), so that the motion sequence can adjust in fractions of a second to new voluntary commands, e.g. changes of speed or direction, or react to afferent messages, e.g. avoiding an obstacle.
A few figures should clarify the efficiency of the brain. 100 million bits per second are sent to the brain from the receptors, of which only a fraction are actively processed and the greatest part simply eliminated. One example that everyone knows is the radio. It plays in the background, is not really listened to, but then a special signal comes, e.g. news, traffic report. The filter is activated and we suddenly pay attention to it.

The efficiency of the brain is about 1,000 bits per second. This corresponds to a muscle stimulus of 1,000 Hz/second for the execution of movement detail. For voluntary commands, e.g. the repetition of a movement, the limit is considerably lower at 20 bits per second.
The vegetative nervous system is activated, in parallel with the command of the motor nerves over the skeletal musculature for movement execution, to stimulate the entire cardio-vascular system. This process is called "associated innervation". This associated innervation also takes place when the athlete imagines details of his movement sequence visually before his eyes before a sporting performance or a competition. The possibility of just simulating movement processes instead of performing them can be used to improve coordination and the precision of separate movement sequences.

The simulation possibility lends itself to mental, psychological focusing, e.g. in their race preparation, marathon runners always familiarise themselves with the course profile, which section should be considered easy, and which difficult.

5 Coordination, Mobility, Speed and Strength Training

Reciprocal links between endurance training and the other motor principal demand forms; coordination, flexibility, speed and strength have already been mentioned in the introduction. They will be explained in more detail below.

5.1 Coordination Training for Running Style (Upper Body, Leg/Foot Control)

Good coordination means:

▶ Efficient running style
▶ Optimal muscle use
▶ Optimal energy consumption
▶ Balanced joint loading
▶ Balanced muscle loading

Badly coordinated upper body movement area leads, among other things, to muscle tension in the shoulder and neck areas as well as premature fatigue due to the increased supporting work of the back muscles.

In practice, the opinion is often supported that running style should not and cannot be corrected. This contradicts the fact that coordination is a basic training form, also called "technique training" by many coaches. Performance can only be improved through good coordination of movement. In many sports, e.g. Olympic gymnastics, diving, high jump, etc., coordination training is an integral part of the training programme.

Either the need for coordination training is unknown or the necessary training is too difficult for the majority of runners. Even when watching many world class runners, one is tempted to ask, "How could their performance improve by improving their coordination, or do they just rely on the "self optimisation effect" to prevail over poor running technique?" Incorrect movements due to joint problems cannot usually be corrected.

101

Coordination training means changing a movement pattern in order to optimise the movement flow or separate movements in the direction of movement. The movement pattern is stored in the cerebellum (see Chapter 4.5 "Control of Muscle Activities by the Brain and nervous System").

Changing a movement pattern is more difficult than starting a new one. Many, many training repetitions are needed until a movement pattern is so changed that it remains dominant even under conditions of fatigue.

To change a movement pattern also requires a great deal of concentration. This quality must also be constantly developed, which is why the author, in his introduction, supplements the five "motor demand forms" with that of "concentration".

Concentration is especially difficult for both runners and walkers, as the movement sequences for these sports have become so automatic that unlike many others they can be performed with no concentration at all. Without any particular incentive, concentration on one thought is only possible for about 3 seconds, after which the human brain then unconsciously moves on to the next thought.

Many runners and walkers have coordination weaknesses in the upper body area. In contrast to the almost linear swinging movement of the legs, they rotate their shoulders instead using a deliberate arm action in the direction of movement.

The lack of active arm action always leads to shoulder rotation, which presents a strength component diagonal to the direction of movement and is thus a performance-limiting factor. The rule of thumb is: "The thumb leads the big toe!" Using slow motion video analysis, both the correct action and the arm and thumb-originated rotation movements of the knees and feet can be clearly seen.

An active arm action in the direction of movement, at a working angle of about 45° upwards, avoiding sinking below the level of the belt on the back swing, both support the lifting of the legs and optimally channel all movement segments into a forward movement (see Figures 56 and 57).

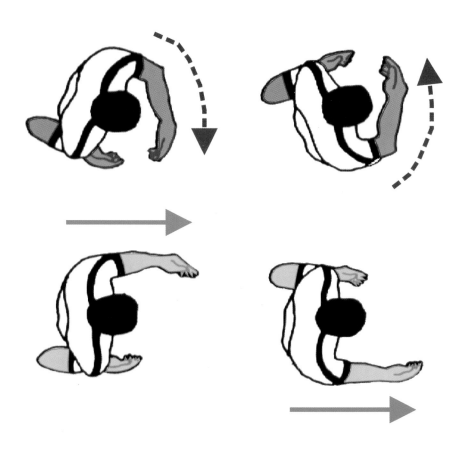

Figure 56: Arm action instead of shoulder rotation. An opposing movement in the upper body must compensate for the swinging movement of the legs. As the legs move almost in a straight line, the corresponding balancing movement in the upper body must do likewise. Such a movement can only be carried out with the arms by swinging from the shoulders. The arms must therefore not rotate in front of the body (left), but must be moved parallel to the body in the direction of movement (right).

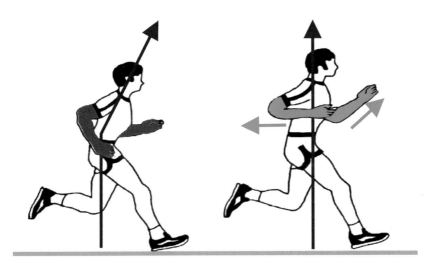

Figure 57: Upper body position and arm action when running and walking.
Left: Many runners let themselves lean forward. This prevents the spine from swinging easily and loosely around the body's centre of gravity, leading to lasting pressure on the vertebrae. If the body is leaning forward, the back muscles must work constantly to maintain a position for which it was not intended, leading to muscle tension and premature tiredness. Deep breathing is also inhibited.
Right: Upright running, head and chin are carried high.
Arm action: the lower arms should not sink below the horizontal, as swinging too low backwards with the arms inhibits leg lift. In the forward movement the lower arm should be brought upwards at an angle of up to 45°, thus optimally supporting the lifting of the legs. The elbows should swing forwards past the body. Both are trainable!

Compensating for these deficits is a tiresome process. Initially, the concentration on a correct arm action slips after the three seconds mentioned above, i.e. after a few strides. The trained athlete remembers this coordination training very few times in a training session. With increased training duration the remembering frequency improves and with it the number of repetitions. 3-12 months are necessary for a lasting movement optimisation. Training partners can help the remembering process during training, as long as the trainee accepts this and doesn't find it too annoying. Regular videoing is neutral and has the advantage

that the trainee can see his own running action and can focus his movement feeling on the correct action (visual input).

The correct arm action is an imperative pre-requisite for a correct leg action. Trying to compensate for the pendulum movement of the legs when walking or running by a rotation in the upper body, leads to a similar rotation movement in the hips and leg area, which can be clearly seen in video analysis.

It should be noted that fast downhill running is only possible by actively moving the arms in the direction of movement with a stabilised upper body.

As far as walking is concerned, especially in Stick and Nordic walking, light, modified ski sticks, similar to cross country ski poles, are used to lengthen the stride and thereby to increase speed. Using the sticks it is even easier to achieve a correct, i.e. forwards-directed arm action. This method is also suggested to runners. Whether or not it works in practice remains to be seen.

Only specific muscle function training can compensate for incorrect leg positions due to muscular imbalances (Figures 42, 43) (see Chapter 4.2 "Muscles and Tendons"). The extension of the hamstring (Figure 44), however, requires a concentrated coordination training programme.

Limping after earlier injuries or operations to the knee and hip joints presents a particularly serious coordination problem. Although the conditions for limping have arisen from the healing process, limping will still occur afterwards, as this movement pattern has become dominant in the cerebellum in the meantime.

Effective coordination training can only be successfully carried out with great concentration and active support from the coach, therapists and video analysis. Periods of more than one year are often necessary. If the limping is not eliminated, in the long term overloading injuries must be expected.

5.2 Flexibility by Stretching and Muscle Strengthening

Good flexibility, i.e. good mobility, means:

▶ Efficient running style
▶ Optimal way of using muscles
▶ Mobile joints
▶ Loose muscles
▶ Good cartilage support
▶ Fast regeneration

Neither walking nor running can train mobility. However, the muscles used become shorter over time due to the monotonous, constantly similar demand (Chapter 4.2 "Muscles and Tendons"). The shortened muscles must be stretched regularly to maintain elasticity and optimal joint movement, as well as to avoid injury [41]. The shortened muscles are stretched by their antagonist (see Figures 38, 40), i.e. both must be of equal strength. The stretching of the shortened muscle and the necessary strengthening of the antagonist can only be achieved by specific, function-orientated exercises [27, 43, 66, 67, 68]. The neglect of this basic training form is the cause of the majority of all back pain.

Alternatives to exercises carried out in the gym or outside are aqua gym or aqua jogging (see Chapter 6.6 "Regeneration – Aquajogging"). The latter is an excellent alternative in case of injury or restricted movement due to arthritis, which require to training to take place without the loading of the weight of the body [3].

To be able to stretch a shortened muscle, i.e. to pull it apart, it must be relaxed (Figure 47 E). Stretching should be slow and held for 20 – 40 seconds, so that the actin and myosin filaments can slide apart (Figure 46). This allows full muscle elasticity and optimal joint mobility to be obtained.

However, if an electrically tense muscle (Figure 47 C/D) is temporarily exposed to a quick, powerful stretch, there is a positive stimulus reaction in the Z disks. Frequent stimulation, if possible in the maximal strength area, enlarges the Z disks and the muscles are strengthened.

5.3   Speed

To what extent the basic motor training forms influence each other is shown by the interaction between speed and endurance. The novice runner can only run very slowly due to his poor endurance ability. As his endurance ability improves, he can run faster. It follows that for speed training in the endurance area, at grass roots level endurance ability must always be improved, e.g. by lengthening the training distance before tempo can be increased, in order to prevent training from being carried out in the anaerobic area. Running speed is the product of "stride length times stride rate". The stride length at grass roots level is 0.80 – 1.20 m. At elite level, it can increase to about 2.20 m. I.e., lengthening the stride inevitably increases running speed. When the stride rate remains the same, the number of strides per minute is increased every time the stride length is extended already the movement speed of each leg. A change or increase in the stride rate is connected with a change in the running rhythm, i.e. the remembered movement programme (see chapter 4.5 "Control of Muscle Activities by the Brain and the nervous System") and is thus very difficult. It cannot be achieved without completely changing the training structure and normally entails a temporary drop in performance. At competition level, "fartlek" (speed play) is carried out to improve speed. This is running with varying loads (speed or incline) and/or tempo running on the track. A proven idea in these cases is to increase speed very slightly and to maintain increased load for as long as possible (1,000 – 3,000 m). Training should be carried out with a heart rate monitor and be supervised so that it is carried out below the aerobic/anaerobic threshold (Figure 26). Training should be carried out at the following intensities in terms of lactate (L) and heart rate (HR):

65% at L < 3 mmol/l and HR < 75% HR $_{max}$
25% at L = 3-4 mmol/l and HR = 75-85% $_{max}$
10% at L > 3-4 mmol/l and HR > 85% HR $_{max}$

Speed is influenced not by endurance ability alone, but also by the optimal coordination of all separate movements in the direction of running, concentration on the extension of the legs and an aggressive toe off.

5.3.1   Basic Speed

Basic speed is genetically predetermined, as already explained in Chapter 4.2.3 "Red and white Muscle Fibres". However, it must be activated by training in children and young people.I repeat that the low lactate tolerance of these age groups must always be taken into consideration. A lack of basic speed cannot be overcome by hard work.

5.3.2　Pace Judgement/Fast Pace Maintenance

It is possible to learn pace judgement. For this you need a measured distance with markers 500 m apart if possible. With a stopwatch and a heart rate monitor, heart rate can be set according to running speed, which then forms the basis for training and competition planning

Fast pace maintenance is easier to train in a race than in training, due to the increased motivation. Sufficient warm-up before the race is absolutely essential for maximal performance.

5.4　Strength Training

Sufficient strength means:

▶　Optimal muscle strength use
▶　Easy management of uneven running surfaces and hills
▶　Muscle balance: agonist – antagonist
▶　Even joint loading
▶　Support: tendons – ligaments – joints
▶　Good body posture

Compared to many other sports, strength does not play a major part in endurance running. That is certainly also the reason why the need for strength training, e.g. in the form of specific strengthening exercises, is underestimated and therefore neglected. One of the most important goals of strength training is to maintain muscle balance. The muscle opponents, agonist and antagonist, or flexor and extensor, can only be balanced by strengthening the weaker one and not by stretching the too-strong partner.

Like the other training forms, strength training must be lifelong, i.e. even in old age [5, 15, 39]. A muscle that is not developed will deteriorate. Anyone who has had to immobilise an arm or a leg due to injury knows how quickly the muscle starts to deteriorate and how tiresome it is to retrain the muscle afterwards.

To have enough strength at old age provides quality of life, as it is needed for climbing stairs, carrying shopping bags or boxes, lifting of objects in the home.

6 Benefits and Risks of Endurance Training

6.1 Positive Effects of Endurance Training

Running is the simplest and most effective form of endurance training. The training volume when cycling must be doubled to achieve the same cardio-vascular effects. Loading stimuli of the muscles when walking are actually sufficient to counteract, for example, the many illnesses caused by lack of exercise.

For a noticeable cardio-vascular activation (e.g. strengthening of the heart muscle), the muscle mass normally used in walking (< 1/7 of the skeletal muscles) is too low to be effective [38]. The most important positive effects on the cardio-vascular system are assembled in Table 1 on page 112 [1, 2, 38, 42, 48, 49, 71].

Additional positive adaptation effects are:

▶ The flow of blood to the heart muscle improves due to the increase, enlargement and opening up of the coronary artery, i.e. the fine arterial capilliaries.
▶ The deep, whole lung breathing improves CO_2-oxygen exchange as a prerequisite for an optimal oxygen uptake of the blood.
▶ There is an improvement in the oxygen binding capacity of the blood (haemoglobin) as well as in the oxygen release (oxygen emission) into the muscle cells.
▶ Venous activity improves. This counteracts cramping.
▶ Alongside strengthening of the leg and back muscles, regular running (as least twice a week) also strengthens the connective tissue, so that the dreaded cellulitis (orange peel skin) is reduced or even eliminated, particularly in the bottom and thighs.
▶ Certain poisons, especially heavy metals, e.g. lead, are eliminated from the body by sweating – like in the sauna. There the circulation is stressed; running trains it instead.

	Untrained (normal)	Trained (good performance level)
Heart Size	About 300	Up to 500 g
Heart Volume M W	About 750 About 550	About 1,200 ml About 1,000 ml
Heart Volume by Body weight man Body weight woman	11.0 9.5	20.5 ml/kg 20.5 ml/kg
Heart rate at rest	70	40-50 beats/minute
Heart rate range	70 – 200	40 – 200 beats/minute
Blood production at rest 　　Per pulse 　　Per minute 　　Per hour	70 0.070 5 300	100-125 ml 0,1-0,125 l 5 l 300 l
Under loading 　　Per minute 　　Per hour	70 – 200 5-24	100-200 ml 5-40 l
Blood volume	5-6	6-8 l
O_2 utilization	Low	Maximal
O_2 uptake	3,300	Up to 6,000 ml/minute
Carbohydrate deposits	Normal	Increased
Fatty acid deposits	Minimal	Maximal
Mitochondria	Normal	increased

Table 1: Effects of long standing endurance training on the cardio-vascular system.

These general statements are also mentioned in the Darmstadt survey. There it can be clearly seen that typical illnesses due to lack of exercise have been reduced by "exercise therapy running" in many runners over the years (see Figure 58).

Along with the medical benefits there is an equally important psychological one: the relaxation effect. Physical exercise activates body and brain cells, warms up the muscles and the good blood flow improves oxygen supply. At the same time, beta endorphins are produced, whose euphoric effect leads to a reduction of stress, problems, bad moods, etc. One runner has summed up the relaxation effect in the following words: "Even if I am very stressed, after one hour of gentle running in the forest, I am relaxed, peaceful and no longer take out my bad moods on my children or my wife."

This statement is also supported by the above-mentioned study, where more than 90% of the participants admit to being happier, more relaxed and balanced after one hour of endurance training. The rest are not, as they constitute the "over ambitious" group, who set themselves unrealistic goals. Consequently they are disappointed in themselves after training when they do not reach their goal (again) and more frustrated than before.

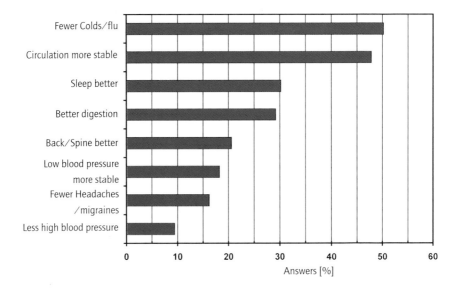

Figure 58: Changes in physical health after several years of endurance training [18].

A further positive effect is that many runners who did hardly any sport at school, and none at all in their 20s, suddenly discover in their 40s and 50s that running is not only fun, but that that they are actually good at it.

6.1.1 Immune System

Regular endurance training strengthens the immune system of the human body [26, 32, 44, 57, 59]. The clear drop in cold-type illnesses in Figure 58 [18] shows this. Even with cancer, it is possible to strengthen the immune system so much that further outbreaks of the disease can be stopped. The prerequisite for this is, though, that training is carried out in the aerobic metabolism, especially in the aerobic fat metabolism.

The individual limit value of about 80% of the maximal performance ability seems to be the threshold above which the strengthening of the immune system becomes an overload instead. For example, after the heavy loading of a marathon, there is a reduced resistance to colds.

That is why after a cold, especially after a virus infection, only light endurance training in the regeneration area (see Figure 26) should be carried out, in order to strengthen the immune system that must fight the disease pathogens in the body, instead of overloading it. In the case of cancer, even when it has been kept under control over many years by endurance training, by crossing the 80% threshold you run the risk of destabilising the immune system. It doesn't matter if this is by running, cycling, etc.

6.1.2   Running during Pregnancy

Pregnancy represents a temporary but profound change in the female body. Opinions as to whether sport and endurance training may or should be continued are still contradictory even today. In recent years, knowledge of the changes in the body of the mother-to-be has advanced so much that even most gynaecologists and midwives could be convinced of the positive effects on the pregnancy of doing sport [28, 61].

The cardio-vascular system of the future mother is increasingly put under pressure through the formation of a second vascular system and through the weight of the child. Endurance training in the aerobic loading area (60-80% of the maximal performance ability) strengthens the cardio-vascular system for these tasks. The oxygen uptake and thus the oxygen supply of the foetus are increased.

In the quoted literature [28, 61], as well as in the secondary literature mentioned there, today the unanimous opinion is that in a normal pregnancy, all aerobic sports are recommended, since they increase physical performance ability, reduce stress and prevent the formation of thrombosis, cramps, haemorrhoids, etc. On the other hand, sports that involve a danger of kicking or falling, as well as extreme endurance loads, e.g. marathon, triathlon, should not be carried out during this period.

Up to which point before the birth the naturally slower and slower endurance training can be carried out is different for each individual. However, it is important that when it is resumed after the birth, endurance training is very slow, as the overstretched pelvic muscles must initially be strengthened again by intensive pelvic floor exercises.

6.2 Physical Check-up before starting Training

In 1974, when the German Sports Federation started the Fun Running movement, it recommended that everyone over 40 should consult a doctor before taking up running as a safety measure. This demand is also repeated every now and then by doctors. In daily practice such a simple recommendation has proved to be unnecessary. There is also the fact that it is only really worthwhile when a very thorough sports-medical exercise test is carried out, and even this offers no guarantee that existing health threats are really found.

In well-founded cases, e.g. very high blood pressure, diabetes, acute complaints, obesity, a visit to a doctor with as positive an attitude to sport as possible is recommended. This can also be an orthopaedist. Under certain preconditions, cycling or swimming can be more suitable forms of exercise and endurance training due to the reduced load on the joints.

In the case of feverish colds, flu or gastro-intestinal infections, you may not run but only walk. After the infection has subsided, it is sensible to rest for two or three days and then to resume *light* training.

6.3 Risks of Cold, Heat, Humidity and Ozone

Whether cold or hot conditions present a special loading or performance limiting factor depends on the personal constitution of the individual. One athlete feels good in cold weather at temperatures below T = 20 °C. For him, high temperatures present a cardio-vascular load that should be taken into account particularly in races and must possibly be suspended by copious drinking. This kind of athlete must take special care in warm, humid conditions and in temperatures above T = 30 °C.

Athletes who produce their best performances in temperatures of T = 20 °C and above are not generally in danger on the cardio-vascular side.

6.3.1 Endurance Competitions at high Temperatures

At high temperatures, in particular, when these are coupled with high physical loading such as a marathon, the body reacts by sweating intensively to cool the surface of the body, especially in the head area. Overheating in the head area leads to extreme performance breakdown, as the author, being a "cold weather runner" knows from experience.

When sweating, the body does not only lose water, but also electrolytes, in particular sodium, calcium, magnesium, etc. Losses of this kind e.g. in a marathon can disturb the electrolyte balance so much in the thigh and calf muscles that they can cause premature exhaustion and/or muscle cramps. An additional intake of electrolyte drinks before and especially during the race is essential in order to maintain performance ability.

The water loss from the blood thickens the blood, leading to an increase in blood viscosity. The heart must beat stronger and react with a faster heart rate, resulting in a loss of performance and premature exhaustion.

The body will not tolerate water losses of above about 3% of bodyweight [40], as the increased thickening of the blood can threaten the performance ability of the heart. That is why the body stops sweating and runs the small risk of overheating, including heat stroke.

That is why it is necessary for the water and electrolyte content of the body to take electrolyte drinks as soon as possible, i.e. at the first refreshment station. Two remarks here:

1. In training prior to the race, the endurance athlete must definitely try which drinks, if any he supports under those loads – not all are easily digestible!

2. Water is not sufficient to make up for the fluid loss, as it cannot replace the electrolytes eliminated by sweating.

One tried and tested and above all inexpensive drink, is the combination of 20-30% apple juice and water. Every athlete must find out for himself which, if any, of the vitamin, electrolyte and energy drinks available on the market are better alternatives, there is no magic potion that works for everyone (see Chapter 7.2 "Electrolyte Drinks").

6.3.2 Running in high Ozone Concentrations

Running in high ozone concentrations? There has been no scientific research yet that has demonstrated that ozone has a damaging effect on humans. Indeed, Hollmann shows in studies in São Paulo, Los Angeles and Mexico City [36] where sport was carried out at ozone concentrations of 600-1,000 µg/m³ without any damage being established. In his own research he found performance drops of 10-15% under ozone loads of 400-600 µg/m³.

It is indisputable, though, that ozone concentrations of over 200 µg/m³ can cause eye and mucous membrane problems. These are not caused by the increased ozone volume, but the accompanying weather conditions: very high temperatures, dry and above all very dusty air. Street and grass dust as well as pollen are the real causes.

For the above reasons it is sensible to move training sessions to the morning and evening or even to the swimming pool.

In the same vein, attention is drawn to a study of the Hesse Ministry for Youth, Family and Health from the year 1991 [31], in which the ozone concentrations in the heavily traffic congested city of Darmstadt were compared with those in the "clean air zone" of Fuerth/Odenwald, 30 km distance to Darmstadt (Figure 59). From this study it emerges that the ozone built up during the day in the city of Darmstadt is broken down again in the evening by the same harmful chemicals from which it is made [cf. 17]. In the "clean air zone" of Odenwald there are no harmful evening chemical emissions and the ozone content goes up and down from day to day.

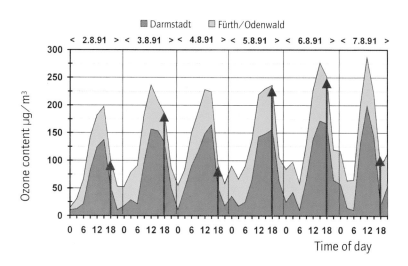

6.4   Risks and Types of Injury

Compared to other sports, running is one of the least dangerous. Reliable injury statistics are not available, as they are only for club athletes, if they exist at all. The author estimates the risk of a serious injury (e.g. muscle fibre, tendon, ligament tears or complete tears, bone or joint injuries) when running as one injury per 10,000 running hours.

Analysis and evaluation [60] of 164 accidents by running club participants showed that stumbling (39%), ankle twists (37% and slipping over (10%) together make up 86% of the types of injury. 38% of participants gave the causes as being distracted and not concentrating. Another 37% make the terrain (uneven = 52%, slippery = 10%, icy = 10%) responsible, not themselves.

However, these figures are relativised by analysis and evaluation according to time of year and time of day: in winter the accident rate at 34% was slightly higher than in summer (25%) and in spring (26%). 64% of all accidents take place during the day and only 24% in the dark.

6.5   Sudden Death while Running

Sudden death when running, despite many sensationalist reports in the press, is rare, but not to be ruled out. Analysis and evaluation of 26 different works on this subject [among others 2, 41, 42] showed that the frequency could only be roughly estimated, as there is no exact data collection. Different authors sometimes come to very different conclusions.

In the running area there are unanimously very low risk values. In an overall analysis of 955 sudden death cases, only 11.4% occurred during sporting activity, and of these only 0.9% when running. In comparison, 16.1% occurred when marching, 8.9% in the sauna, 6.2% when swimming and 4.7% when cycling.

As for training volume, the estimations fluctuate between 130,000 – 360,000 running hours per death. The post mortem results published in the literature have unanimously reflected that for about two thirds of such sudden death cases there are clear health causes, e.g. infections, in particular heart muscle inflammation, acquired or unrecognised, congenital heart and intestinal anomalies, kidney changes and failure.

Figure 59: (left page) Ozone concentrations from 2.8.1991 – 7.8.1991 in the congested city of Darmstadt and the "clean air zone" of Fuerth/Odenwald [31].

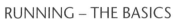
In a series of cases, runners have continued to train with acute organ diseases or virus infections against doctors' advice.

In one third of the cases, there was no evidence of pathological causes. Whether mental stress and risk factors play a role in these cases has not yet been established. For runners such risk factors exist, for example, with regular over-training, i.e. when you regularly run with a group that you can't keep up with.

Stopping every time you can't keep up also means experiencing a feeling of failure each time. In the long term, this leads to the anxiety and worry of "not being good enough" and to distress. In the cardio-vascular system this disrupts the heart rhythm, which in serious cases can develop into a heart murmur.

Based on analyses, authors all agree that most victims must have felt warning signals, e.g. chest or upper stomach pains under loading, undefined pains in the left arm, nausea, etc.

6.6   Regeneration – Aquajogging

Aquajogging means running in the water supported by a buoyant vest or a swimming belt. In contrast to normal running, where he must absorb up to five times his bodyweight on each stride, in aquajogging the body floats without touching the ground. As the bodyweight does not have to be supported, you can run without pain in the tendons, ligaments and joints in the water [3].

Aquajogging was discovered by a Vietnam veteran in the 1970s, who was unable to continue to run due to injury. He started experimenting with water running with a swimming vest, then with a home made swimming belt.

Today, aquajogging has an important role at both grass roots and elite level sport for movement and regeneration training, for example to maintain mobility and fitness in cases of injury or joint arthritis. The training programme in the water should be a complement to the rest of the training programme. The relationship between running and aquajogging has not been conclusively proved in terms of the training stimulus, as no linear connection between the heart rate and the lactate values of both types of training appear to exist [65].

People with high blood pressure should be careful when aquajogging due to the additional pressure of the water. The clearly higher cardio-vascular load can be risky in such cases.

7 Nutrition

Almost no other subject exists on which there are so many different opinions as that of nutrition. There is one basic fact that is true for everyone, though:

▶ If you eat more than you need, you put on weight
▶ If you need more than you eat, you lose weight

It is common knowledge that it is easier to put on weight than to lose it. The body stores every surplus calorie in its fat cells, for the "bad times". Daily practice shows that dieting can empty these to an extent, but not eliminate them. When the diet is stopped, the fat cells of all overweight people unfortunately take every opportunity to top up their lost fat (+ excess load). The exact function of the fat cells is the subject of much research at the moment.

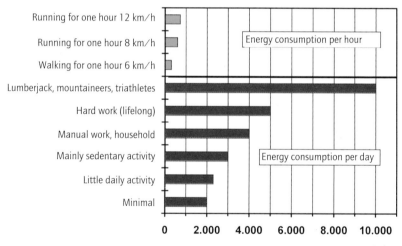

Figure 60: Daily energy consumption of a man weighing 70kg for different activities (bottom of figure) as well as one hour's walking and running training.

121

It is clear, though, how much energy is needed and used in daily life and in sporting activity. In the lower part of Figure 60, the daily energy consumption of a man weighing 70 kg is shown. In the upper part, the consumption is given for one hour's walking and running, which is added to the activity values in the bottom part. This means that someone who works in an office cannot avoid the need for housework with a one-hour run at 12 km/hour. In the weekly comparison, which is the daily one multiplied by seven, the relations are correspondingly worse, if training is not carried out daily – a frustrating balance for many people!

It is possible to reduce the bodyweight by running. At least three training sessions per week are necessary though, one of which must be for at least two hours and at the same time no superfluous calories must be consumed.

Energy consumption depends on movement speed and, according to the laws of physics ($E = \frac{1}{2} Mv^2$), increase with the square of the speed. The curve values in Figure 61 for running and cycling do not obey this law sufficiently, they are averages of various literature statistics and therefore only to be treated as guidelines.

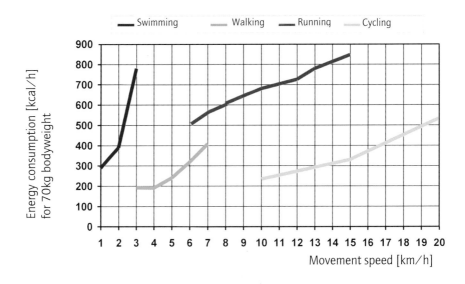

Figure 61: Influence of movement speed on energy consumption when swimming, walking, running and cycling (the values for running and cycling are for guidance only).

Furthermore, there is wide agreement on the nutrition composition for sportspeople in terms of carbohydrate, fat and protein. It depends on the strength component of the sport concerned (see Figure 62). In the strength sports, protein plays a very important role as a cell builder. In endurance sports, carbohydrates at a ratio of 60% are required as main energy provider [64]. Putting into practice these food requirements appears to be difficult for many sportspeople.

Further basic principles are:

▶ It is better to eat little and often than a lot a few times. The stomach gets used to small portions
▶ If you chew slowly, you feel full sooner than if you eat fast.
▶ The *hungry* eyes that can often make you eat more than you need can only be satiated by reason. Slow eating helps here too.
▶ The time of day also plays a role: more in the morning and at lunchtime, less in the evening. Everything that is not used up in the evening, the body keeps back for *hard times* – which is where the cushions of fat come from.
▶ Abundant fruit and vegetables as vitamin and fibre rich and low calorie nutrition.

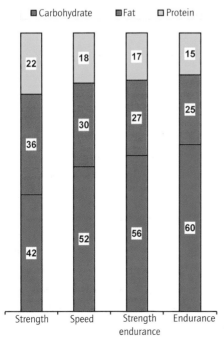

Note:
The consumption of performance-enhancing and pain-killing agents and medicine is widespread even in popular sport and is still a doping offence.

Figure 62: Food composition in terms of carbohydrate, fat and protein for sports with varying strength components [64].

7.1 Tips for Food Composition

A well-balanced mixed diet without particular supplements, but with food that is a fresh as possible, is the basis for healthy nutrition. It is easier than ever before to manage this, as **fresh (!)** fruit and vegetables are available year-round, i.e. not in the processed form as marmalade, canned vegetables, etc. With fresh products and the wide range of meat, fish and cereal products, the vitamin, mineral and trace element needs can usually be covered.

In the choice of food, attention should not only be paid to the rough allocation in terms of carbohydrate, fat and protein content, but crucially, to the trace elements they contain and the breakdown speed (bioavailability) too.

Examples for carbohydrates:

Per 100g	kcal	CH g	Na mg	K mg	Mg mg	Ca mg	Fe mg
Rye bread	209	43	425	290	45	45	3
White bread	244	50	540	130	25	60	1
Unpolished rice	348	75	10	150	155	25	3
Polished rice	347	78	6	105	65	6	1

CH Carbohydrate, Na Sodium, K Potassium, Mg Magnesium, Ca Calcium, Fe Iron, B$_1$ Vitamin B$_1$, C Vitamin C

Wholemeal products (wholemeal bread, wholemeal pasta, brown rice, etc) are broken down considerably more slowly than processed grains (white bread, "normal" pasta, polished rice, etc). The slower carbohydrate breakdown in wholemeal products has the advantage of making the energy available in the body for longer and more evenly.

Examples for the ingredients of muesli

Per 100g	kcal	CH g	Fat g	Na mg	K mg	Mg mg	Ca mg	Fe mg	B$_1$ mg	C mg
Rye grain	266	54	2	40	510	120	65	5	0,4	
Wheat grain	302	60	2	8	500	145	45	3	0,5	
Oat flakes	364	62	7	5	335	140	55	5	0,6	
Wheat bran	195	23	5	2	1390	590	45	4	0,7	
Hazel nuts	648	9	62	2	635	155	225	4	0,4	3
Walnuts	670	12	63	2	545	130	85	3	0,3	3
Almonds	598	9	54	5-40	835	170	250	4	0,2	1-6
Bananas	90	20	<1	1	395	35	9	<1		12
Apples	50	11	<1	3	145	6	7	<1		12
Fresh figs	62	13	<1	2	240	20	55	<1		3
Dried figs	272	62	1	40	850	70	165	3,3	0,1	3
Milk 3.5%	66	5	4	50	155	12	120			2
Yoghurt 3.5%	69	4	4	50	155	12	120			2

CH Carbohydrate, Na Sodium, K Potassium, Mg Magnesium, Ca Calcium, Fe Iron, B$_1$ Vitamin B$_1$, C Vitamin C

Low fat milk and low fat yoghurt differ from the full cream products only in their fat content.

There is no limit to individual taste preferences in the composition of muesli. Even if nuts and almonds contain a very high proportion of fat, they are excellent sources of minerals.
In commercially produced muesli and energy bars, be careful of the various carbohydrate and fat contents. They are suitable as short-term energy providers and after prolonged sporting activity. Whether or not they can be consumed during the activity depends on the sport and the individual prerequisites – one person needs it, another cannot support eating during activity.

The uptake (resorption) of iron from vegetable products is very low. Meat products are recommended here, especially pig liver.

Tip: **Women** should regularly have their iron levels tested, not just for haemoglobin levels, but also for stored iron [33]. Iron deficiency is very frequently the cause of an unexplained drop in performance.

7.2 Electrolyte Drinks

Under normal living conditions, sufficient electrolyte quantities are provided by the diet. In the case of high physical loading, in particular, when intensive sweating is involved and at high temperatures, the intake of additional electrolyte drinks is sensible and necessary in order to maintain performance levels. The body loses potassium, calcium, magnesium, etc when it sweats, which must be replaced as quickly as possible, e.g. in the form of mineral water, diluted apple juice, mineral drinks, meat broth, unsweetened or lightly sweetened tea, etc. [12, 50, 58].

The magnesium and calcium content of the mineral water should be as high as possible (Mg > 100 mg/l, Ca > 250 mg/l), and the sodium content as low as possible (Na < 50 mg/l).

Diluted apple juice – also called apple juice spritzer – a mixture of 1/3 apple juice and 2/3 (mineral) water, is a good and inexpensive alternative to the prepared commercial drinks due to the use of pure, natural apple juice. Which, if any, of the many vitamin, electrolyte and energy drinks available on the market are a better alternative is up to individual athletes to try for themselves – there is no magic potion. NB: Most of the commercially prepared juices contain unnecessarily high amounts of sugar.

If you only run for an hour once or twice a week, and replace lost fluids with mineral water or apple juice spritzers, endurance training will not cause an additional electrolyte requirement.

On particularly hot days, as a precautionary measure, it is even advisable to drink 0.5-1 litre of fluid before running, according to taste and digestibility, still mineral water, apple juice spritzer, tea, mineral drinks, etc. In long training sessions, the magnesium supply is particularly jeopardised. Magnesium is one of our most important electrolytes, as it is involved in facilitating about 350 processes, especially in the control and supply of muscles. Muscle cramps, particularly when they occur at night after an intensive endurance training session, are caused by a magnesium deficiency.

Magnesium is not easily taken up (resorbed) by the body, which is why it is advisable to take only small quantities daily over a long period of time (2-3 months). As a rough rule of thumb, if the amount is doubled, only 20% more will be taken up by the body and the rest will be eliminated as "expensive" urine. As the author himself can testify, a known side-effect of an overdose is diarrhoea. Magnesium is not a doping agent and is available in every pharmacy.

7.3   Beer and other alcoholic Drinks

Along with many nutrients and electrolytes, beer also contains 3.5-6% alcohol. It is appreciated by many sportspeople as a thirst-quencher after training. However, the harder the preceding training session, the stronger the alcoholising effect seems to be. Only small amounts are sufficient to lengthen regeneration times and to diminish physical efficiency.

One glass of wine a day, particularly red wine, is reputed, particularly in French literature, to have life-extending effects. The author would not like to comment on the extent of scientific evidence for this. It is certain, though, that large amounts, as well as indulgence in "hard" alcoholic drinks, are performance-limiting factors.

7.4   Diets

Dieting and running? This question is of concern mainly to women, as they experiment more with diets than men do. **Particular care should be taken with the crash-diet (no-calorie-diet) + running**, which many female runners mistakenly think will give an optimal weight loss.

It only rarely works, for where can the energy for running come from, when the energy stores are empty due to the crash-diet (can a car work without petrol)? The author has noticed at the running club that female runners following the crash-diet have to stop after half an hour and even faint. They are simply burnt out. This is particularly true for novice female runners who only have very low energy deposits available.

Care should be taken with all diets, in which certain foods are unilaterally withheld or even withdrawn. These include, among others, diuretic and slimming teas. These diets can often deprive the body of important minerals like potassium, calcium, magnesium, etc. Very little is yet known about the interaction of these minerals, except that efficient muscle function depends on their existing in balanced proportion.

8   Clothing

What's **underneath** is more important than what's **on top**. For running the best materials for underwear are pure cotton – for women including knickers – or micro fibre. Cotton soaks up sweat well and reduces the danger of chafing under the armpits and especially the nipples – a problem encountered by both men and women.

Micro fibres bring the sweat to the outside and leave the skin dry. This reduces the unpleasant cold feeling caused by clothes that are wet with sweat. If several layers of clothing are worn on top of each other, they must fit well together. The more the athlete sweats, the more important it is!

Clothing should be loose and airy. The loose fit prevents too much heat loss. T-shirts and sweatshirts should be made of cotton or micro fibre. Micro fibre leggings or Gore-Tex jackets have now replaced the good old tracksuit made of man-made fibre. Jackets should have a hood and a zip fastener at the front that can be opened or closed as required. At least one pocket must have a zip in which to keep car and house keys safe.

Nylon anoraks are only a good protection against the cold in strong winds, particularly when running in the open countryside. In the rain, the author considers a normal training jacket to be better than a nylon anorak, as condensation can easily build up underneath it! It is important to be and stay warm when running, but the sauna is the best place for a sweating cure, when running it is not beneficial. Sweating means water loss, but no real weight loss; it just costs more strength than necessary and also means that more valuable salts are lost than necessary.

It is advisable to dress more warmly in training than in competition, as the body generates more warmth in energy transfer due to the higher performance level in a competitive race. In summer in temperatures of above 20 °C: shorts and short-sleeved t-shirts or vest. Below 10 °C - long trousers and sweatshirts. When the thermometer drops below zero, gloves, hat and long johns are not a bad idea. If the temperature drops further, it can be appropriate to wear a scarf over the mouth for the first quarter of an hour to warm up the inhaled air. Afterwards, the body will warm up the air temperature in advance, so that it is warm enough to breathe in.

Attention should also be given to socks. Each individual must find the fibre that suits him best. Some wear only cotton, others prefer mixed fibres and others again swear by towelling socks, and label their socks "right" and "left" so that they can put the correct one on the correct foot.

8.1   Clothing for Running in the Dark

If you have to run in the dark – which is often unavoidable during the winter months – should wear **snow-white** outer clothing, so that you can be seen by oncoming traffic as soon as possible and not crashed into. Think about this next time you buy a training jacket, as white jackets are often only available in spring or summer months. Alternatively you could wear a white vest over a dark t-shirt or sweatshirt. As the human eye cannot perceive colours very well in the dark, yellow or orange-coloured outer clothing are interpreted as "grey" and, because of its poor light reflecting ability, it is darker for the human eye than white clothing!

If you must run on roads with traffic, you should definitely wear reflecting bands on your arms, legs and on your back. The blinking lights used by some runners are a good idea for lone runners, if worn in a group they irritate other runners.

Always take a small torch with you.

9 Shoes

The good old gym shoe of twenty years ago has today become a sometimes even over-sophisticated high-tech product. Compared to the '80s, we no longer just speak of "good" or "bad" shoes, but "suitable" or "unsuitable" models for individuals. Most running shoes are just meant for walking. The manufacture of special walking shoes is more than anything just a marketing ploy.

There are currently about 300 running shoes on the market, which can be divided roughly into four categories, for which each manufacturer chooses a different name:

1. Competition model: racing, lightweight
2. Light training model: lightweight trainer, cushion
3. Supporting training model: stable-cushion, stability, support, and motion control
4. Cross-country/winter model: off-road, trail

But which one is right for you? Qualified scientific advice is the exception and only to be found in specialist shops. Even for the specialists it is very difficult to have an overview of all the available models, as the manufacturers change their ranges two or three times a year.

To complicate matters even further, manufacturers often give an existing name to a completely new shoe, which is different in every detail from its predecessor. Manufacturers refer to these cases as "further development". But such things have little to do with development or even progress. The designer has suddenly thought of something new and it's up to the runner to experiment with the new shoe to see if and how it works.

A consequence of the lack of advice is that runners are wearing shoes that are not right for them not only at grass roots level but also at elite level. How often that happens can be seen when the feet of the participants in fun runs and marathon races are observed not from the front but from behind.

Wearing the wrong shoes wastes both strength and time. It is frequently the cause of unexplained overloading injuries (see Figure 51). That's why the exact functions and properties of shoes are examined in the following sections and in Chapter 9.2 "Tips for buying Shoes".

9.1 Functions and Properties of Running Shoes

The running shoe is the runner's most important "piece of clothing" [16, 21]. It too must follow the laws of physics, which state that every action has an equal and opposite reaction. That means that every force that acts on it and the ground simultaneously acts on the body and thus the muscles, tendons, ligaments and joints. As the behaviour of the shoes during this transfer of force decisively influences the entire skeletal system and thus the health:

▶ The shoe is the link between the body and the ground.
▶ All mechanical forces enter the body via the shoes.
▶ The shoe influences the physical structure.
▶ Incorrect loading caused by shoes damage the health.

When walking, on each stride the bodyweight loads the shoes with 40-100 kg per stride. When running this increases according to running speed to from two to five times bodyweight. For an average running speed, the shoe is loaded with about three times bodyweight, i.e. for a runner weighing 70 kg; this means a load of 210 kg per stride. These loads must be taken into account. A shoe that is too soft for one runner, i.e. a shoe with too little stability, inevitably provokes postural defects, particularly an inward bend called pronation (see Figure 63 left).

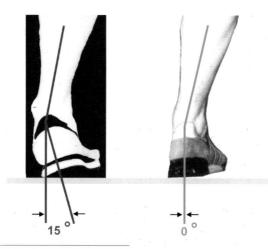

Figure 63: Left: overpronation caused by shoes that are too weak. Right: the same runner in a shoe with suitable support.

9.1.1 Life Expectancy

Not only do shoes that are too weak provoke postural defects right from the start, but also those with a soft mid sole or badly worn heels (Figure 64). With a stride length of 1.00 m, there are 500 loads per kilometre on the right and left shoes. Good shoes last about 1,000 km or 500,000 loads. Many do not. The author has known enough examples in the area of "softies" that have become uncontrollably deformed after only 50 – 100 km.

The wearing down of a shoe normally takes place slowly and is hardly noticed by the runner – it is insidious. The more it is worn down, the more incorrect the loading, leading one day to overloading reactions in the muscles, tendons, ligaments or joints.

Pain warning signals always mean that something is wrong. But only in exceptional cases do runner and doctor trace the source of the pain, e.g. in the knees or back, back to worn down heels or weak heel support in the running shoes.

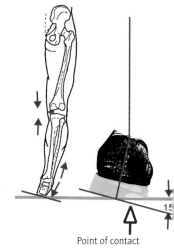

Runners and doctors only rarely know about this relationship. The doctor responsible has no chance of knowing the causes, i.e. the shoe defects. He doesn't normally get to see them.

Usually he doesn't even know that, or how much, his patients runs, as he has only been told the symptoms, i.e. the pain mentioned, not the possible causes (see Figure 64).

Point of contact

Figure 64: A worn-down heel is like running on a steep slope, e.g. of 15°.

The athlete can avoid this by not only checking his training shoes regularly for defects, but also alternating them after each use so as to avoid monotonous (the same every time) incorrect loading. It doesn't matter here if a different model is used each time or another pair of the same model.

As a rule of thumb, for every day of the week that you run, have a different pair of shoes. This doesn't require more shoes in total as each pair can be worn for longer.

9.1.2   Controlling – Supporting – Shock Absorbing

The author has been dealing with the testing and properties of training shoes since the 70s [19, 22], and has formulated the following requirements:

The shoe must:

- ▶ Control the foot perfectly.
- ▶ Support the foot.
- ▶ Absorb the shock of impact.

The shoe must not:

- ▶ Hinder the unwinding movement and toe off force of the foot.

The shoe should:

- ▶ Protect the foot from penetrating stones, dirt and moisture.

9.1.2.1 Controlling

From the first contact with the ground, the shoe takes over the control of the foot. It is crucial in controlling the unrolling movement of the foot from the first heel contact to the last toe off (Figure 65). The correct foot control is a vital prerequisite for an impeccable unrolling action. This calls for a good fit, an impeccable heel fit and correct lacing. The correct shoe controls the foot; the wrong one "leads it astray"!

9.1.2.2 Supporting

Most runners touch down with the outside edge of the heel (Figure 65). The foot then tilts inwards into the support phase. The slower he does that, the lower the stress loads acting on the body.

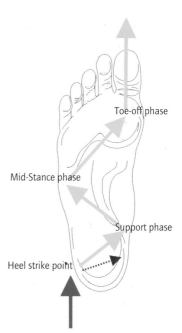

Toe-off phase

Mid-Stance phase

Support phase

Heel strike point

Figure 65: The unrolling path of the foot when touching down with the heel.

The inwards tilting movement is called "pronation". Pronation angles of 0-5° are normal (Figure 66 left: standing barefoot). At angles of 3-5° there is good self-absorption by the foot of the shock load. At larger angles, it becomes over-pronation, which in the long term leads to overloading of the knee and hip joints (see Figure 51).

If a patient goes to see a doctor with such complaints, only in exceptional cases will he be asked to bring along the training shoe has worn most often recently.

If the doctor did this, he would be amazed to see that the pronation angle of his patient, considered normal when barefoot, is doubled when the latter just stands in his too weak, i.e. unstable shoe (Figure 66 centre).

Normal pronation becomes over-pronation. The doctor could only reach the correct assessment after observing the patient running, though, as then the dynamic running load comes into play. This can increase the pronation angle by up to three times (Figure 66 right).

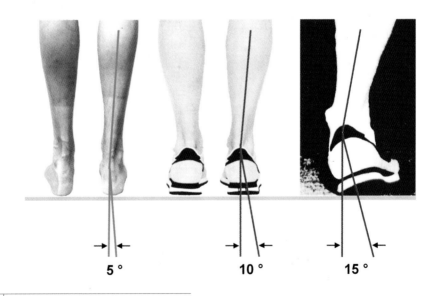

Figure 66: Left: standing barefoot with normal pronation (5°). Centre: even when standing, shoe-related pronation increase of 5-10°. Right: with dynamic load of v = 12 km/h, shoe-related over-pronation (15°).

Astonishingly enough, under these strong defective loads, pains in the spring joint areas are only rarely observed. However, these loads are particularly dangerous for the knee (Figure 51). That is why in the case of knee pain – not just for runners – the condition of the (training) shoe and the foot-shoe combination must always be included in the search for the causes.

It should be pointed out that if heel spur symptoms start to appear, the mobility of the spring joints should be checked, as the pain symptoms are practically identical, but the treatment is completely different.

Over-pronation can be compensated for by support wedges, which are built into the stable models. The choice of a well-supporting shoe has the advantage over a supporting insole that the whole shoe is built to provide support. Supporting insoles require the bottom of the shoe to be firm; they are useless if it is soft! The range of shoes available with support wedges is very wide, ranging from small wedges for light runners with little over-pronation up to extreme models for the overweight with marked over-pronation (see Figure 67). When selecting a shoe, ensure that the support function of a shoe is optimal and not maximal.

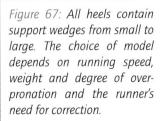

Figure 67: All heels contain support wedges from small to large. The choice of model depends on running speed, weight and degree of over-pronation and the runner's need for correction.

135

9.1.2.3 Shock Absorption

What is shock absorption? Everyone borrows this term from physics. Only a few know its exact definition though. Most people use it – incorrectly – to mean "a pleasant feeling on touch down". Shock absorption in the training shoe means:

Destruction of movement energy (by conversion into heat)

The bottom of the shoe, consisting of a mid sole and a running sole, should absorb the high pressure loads in the touch-down phase, but not impair the body's own muscle elasticity in the thigh and calf muscles. To manage this, the firmness of the training shoe must be suited to individual running conditions, i.e. speed, bodyweight, touch down point, type of ground, etc. [19, 22, 73] (see Chapter 9.1.2.4 "Bodyweight and Running Speed").

In the touch-down phase the body mass acts as an external force on the upper and lower leg musculature. This builds up the body's own elastic potential, while the pre-tensed musculature is stretched in the touch down phase. The energy components are then released and used actively by extending the leg in the toe-off phase. If there are absorption elements built into the sole of the shoe (see Figure 68), they slow down the movement, thereby causing tension to build up in the muscle and the myosin and actin fibres to glide apart (see Figure 47 C/D). NIGG [55, 56, 69] has shown that this can lead to up to a third of muscle elasticity being lost. The model in Figure 68, which is meant for special use, is the right shoe for specific cases, e.g. for an elderly man who has to run very slowly on concrete and where heel strike is in the

middle of the heel not the outside, so that the shoe does not press right down. This does not contradict the basic statement.

To prevent the foot remaining for too long in the support and mid-stance phases due to excess shock absorption (example: Figure 68), a good correspondence between the runner's stride rate and the absorption ability of the shoes is the pre-requisite.

Figure 68: A manufacturer advertises the good shock absorbing performance of one of its models with these photos. But a "spring" pressed right down like this leads to great losses of elasticity in the musculature and simultaneously reduces foot control, since the foot can wobble about in all directions.

The demand for absorption properties is hence called "No destruction of energy by the shoe" [69], so that the kinetic energy potential of the musculature can be used up completely and not lost at a rate of 20-30% per stride, the consequence of which are premature tiredness and bad competition performance.

From this point of view, it would be better to run barefoot, i.e. without shoes. As NIGG has shown, in optimal cases wearing shoes wastes, at least 5% of energy, in the worst case, even 30% or more. The composition of losses and the increased energy demand for the shoe are as follows:

▶ Lifting work for the shoe: 0.1% per 100 g shoe weight
▶ Acceleration work for the shoe: 0.5 – 1.0%
▶ Lifting work for the body's centre of gravity: 1% per 5 mm of sinking
▶ Stabilising work of the joints: 1%
▶ Elastic/visco-elastic losses: 2%

In the advertising, the weight of the shoe is given a significance that, as this research shows, is not at all justified. The lifting work for the shoe amounts to only 0.1% per 100 g shoe weight of the total energy needed. The supporting function of the shoe, however, approaches ten times the importance. To lift the deeper sinking centre of gravity of the body by 5mm in a shoe that is too soft, 0.5 – 1% more energy must be expended (Figure 69). Runners who over-pronate strongly should be aware of this. Daily practice shows that many of them sink at least 1cm in their too weak (racing) shoes. Their performances suffer as a result of their mistaken choice of shoes.

In the same vein, the brand marketing slogan "energy return", should be investigated briefly. A return of the pushing force which the body delivers into the heel contact area as it touches down must be directed forwards in the sole of the shoe into the toe-off area in order to be effective. There is as yet no technical solution for such an impulse continuation. The sole of the shoe is constructed to absorb shock and causes the opposite!

Per 5 mm: 0.5-1%
more lifting work

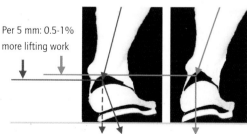

Figure 69: 5 mm sinking of the bodyweight due to shoe-related over-pronation uses up 0.5-1% more energy – that leads to premature tiredness and costs time in a competition.

9.1.2.4 Bodyweight and Running Speed

In shoe tests or brochures, a difference is often made between slow and fast and light and heavy runners. There is, as yet, no definite, general classification. The author differentiates as follows:

Slow runners:	> 6 min/km, fast runners:< 6 min/km
Light runners:	< 65 kg, heavy runners: > 80 kg

Runners load the shoe when they touch down with energy (E), which, when calculated from their body mass (M) and their running speed (v) gives the following formula:

$$E = \frac{1}{2} * M * v^2 \ [M = \text{body mass in kg, } v = \text{running speed in m/s}]$$

From this formula it follows that:

1. Body mass (M):   the mass produces a linear load increase, i.e. double the mass produces double the load.

2. Running speed (v):   the load on the running shoe increases with the square of the velocity. This means that a doubling of the speed quadruples the load!

The sample calculations in Table 2 should show how greatly the running speed affects the demands on the shoe.

Mass:

1: M = 50 kg
2: M = 100 kg

Running speed:

1: v = 6 km/hour   = 10 min/km = 1.7 m/s = beginners' speed

2: v = 12 km/hour   = 5 min/km   = 3.3 m/s = trained athlete
                                                                    (e.g. marathon 3:30 h)

3: v = 18 km/hour   = 3.3 min/km = 5.0 m/s = highly trained
                                                                    (e.g. marathon 2:20 h)

Example Mass/speed	Mass M kg	Running speed v m/s	Energy $(1/2 * M * v^2)$ kg m^2/s^2	Loading factor
1.	50	1.7	69.4	1
Mass doubled	100	1.7	138.9	2
2.	50	1.7	69.4	1
Speed doubled	50	3.3	277.8	4
Speed tripled	50	5.0	625.0	9
3.	50	1.7	69.4	1
Mass doubled and speed tripled	100	5.0	1250.0	18

Table 2: Load: connection between running speed and body mass.

Even if he is overweight, the slow running beginner loads his training shoes substantially less than the trained athlete, due to his slower running speed (see above). The higher the running speed and the higher the mass, the firmer and more stable the shoes must be.

When buying shoes in a shop, they may not feel as comfortably soft as the feeling when standing and walking will suggest or as the advertising recommends.

9.1.2.5 Heel-Strike, Mid-stance and Toe-off Phases

As the example of a loading model (Figure 65) presented by Cavanagh [13] shows, in the heel strike phase (see Figure 70) a force peak is built up in the rear of the foot that pushes the body off the ground. The shorter this period is (sketched in Figure 65), the harder is the shoe, and the longer it is, the smaller the pushing effect. The standing phase is the neutral phase, in terms of the force direction. It is reached after a good third of the total ground contact time.

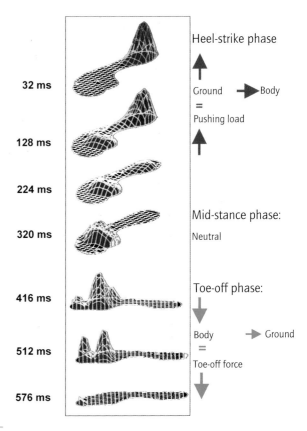

Figure 70: Within 32 ms of the heel-strike phase a force peak builds up in the heel that pushes the body off the ground. The shorter this period is, the harder the shoe, the slower it is, the better the shock absorption. Then a shift takes place from the rear to the front of the foot with a simultaneous change in the force direction. After 416 ms, the toe-off force in the ball of the foot reaches its maximum. It is crucial for the running speed that this force can be transferred immediately into an impulse for the next stride and not diminished by shock absorbing elements in the sole of the front of the shoe.

While for the running shoe it doesn't matter from which point the pressure load is released – it works on the shoe in the same way from above as from below – in the human body, the pushing load in the heel-strike phase in the rear of the foot (pushing direction from the ground to the body) must be clearly differentiated from the toe-off force in the toe-off phase in the front of the foot (pressure direction from the body to the ground). The pushing loads that act on the body must be absorbed. The running shoe manufacturers use various absorption systems for this (air, gel, honeycomb cushioning, etc.) An alternative suggestion from the author "run softly with a hard shoe", i.e. use the muscles' own elasticity fully at 70-80% of maximal speed.

To absorb toe-off forces, i.e. to reduce them, is nonsense from the point of view of physics, it costs the runner strength and time! However, an entire industry does this and incorporates air, gel and honeycomb cushions, etc. An academic study, which cannot be quoted for advertising reasons, has shown this in great detail.

The argument that such shock absorbing elements were good for front foot or middle foot runners is likewise not tenable. These people have no such requirements, as the body's own shock absorbing mechanisms during heel-strike are sufficient due to other biomechanical laws of leverage.

9.1.2.6 Flexibility in the Forefoot Area of the Shoe

The running shoe should ensure an impeccable unrolling action in the front of the foot. For this, both firmness and flexibility are required. This is not a contradiction. Firmness is provided by the mid-sole.

Flexibility, i.e. the fold line of the shoe in the area of the ball of the foot is determined by the shape of the running sole and/or by two or three narrow slits in the mid-sole.

If the sole is too stiff, the foot is levered away over the ball of the foot and at the same time the force transfer from the foot to the ground is reduced. A sole that is inflexible in the forefoot area is only the correct alternative for stiffened first toe joints that cannot and should not be moved any longer, in order to run without pain.

Mid-soles that are too soft reduce the force transfer from the foot to the ground and impair direction stability in the toe-off phase. The firm sole structure in the forefoot also has the task of protecting the foot from sharp stones.

9.2   Tips for Buying Shoes

Laughing or crying?

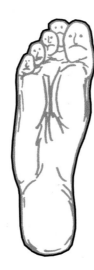

Mistaken buys cannot be completely avoided, even with the advice of experienced experts. However, the risk can be reduced to a minimum by thinking about it beforehand and checking of the fit. Before making a purchase, the following questions should be answered:

A question of chosing the correct shoe!

1. What sort of running shoe do I want: training and long racing distance (above 10 km) or short racing distance (up to 10 km)?
2. Which surface will I use them on: road (asphalt), on level and firm, or on uneven and gravelly paths, in the wet, the snow and/or ice?
3. Which kind of shock absorption and foot control should the model have and which load (running speed/bodyweight) must the shoe withstand?
4. Do I have an incorrect gait that should be taken into account, e.g. pronation?
5. What makes a correct-fitting shoe?
6. Where do I get qualified advice, e.g. treadmill analysis?
7. What experiences did I have with my previous shoes?
8. Price – how much must I pay for my running shoes?

9.2.1 Training/Racing

It is obvious that racing models should not be worn for training, as support and foot control are normally lower. However, very good training shoes can also be worn for racing. The superior support and foot control mean that the runner tires later, which is particularly noticeable over longer (> 10 km) distances. The longer the distance, the firmer (not harder) the shoe must be and the better it must control the foot in order to avoid premature tiredness.

For faster races over shorter distances, the shoe should be very firm in the forefoot area, to ensure maximal power transfer from the shoe to the ground. Soft mid soles or shock absorbing cushions always mean time and power are lost.

9.2.2 Running Surfaces

The majority of running shoes is specifically constructed for the running conditions in the USA, ten times the size of the other running markets, i.e. for road running. These models have in common little support and are only just about suitable for the used forest and country trails mainly in Europe, as, e.g. on the slopes or bends, loading can be doubled. In addition, these models often do not offer enough protection from sharp stones in the forefoot area.

In Germany, 66% of all running is done on uneven country, firm and woodland trails, while in the USA flat asphalt and concrete predominate. These differences in usage also explain why certain running shoes do well in shoe tests in the USA yet the same models are considered unsuitable for German running conditions.

Shoes that are designed for uneven surfaces can also be worn without problem on the road. The cross-country and off-road models are mainly suitable for the special ground features of extremely uneven surfaces.

N.B. The term "cross training shoe" does not refer to cross-country running, but to all-round training for use **across** all sports.

Wet surfaces: On wet asphalt, fine profiles grip better than thick ones, for wet terrain, thick studs are more appropriate.

9.2.3 Loading

How stable the shoe must be depends on the running speed, the bodyweight and the question of whether pronation must and should be compensated for. Again, this should be optimal and not maximal. Over-correction leads to incorrect loading just as inadequate correction does.

9.2.4 Criteria of a good Fit

You should proceed as follows. However, the author knows that the psychological components, such as preferred brand, appearance and price, cannot be completely left out.

- ▶ Last shape
- ▶ Toe length/ball of foot fold line
- ▶ Shoe length (foot + 1cm)
- ▶ Toe room/width
- ▶ Heel fit/hold
- ▶ Ankle freedom of movement
- ▶ Lacing

9.2.4.1 Last Shape

There is a difference between straight and curved lasts, which can be easily established by looking at the shoe from underneath and removing the insole.

Racing models are usually extremely curved, nearly always in fact. However, the author is not yet acquainted with the biomechanical justification for this.

Slightly curved lasts suit the overwhelming majority of people in central Europe. The lasts of most extremely stable shoes are straight.

9.2.4.2 Ball of Foot Folding Line

There are runners with very short toes, and others with very long toes (Figure 71). Consequently, the ball of the foot folding line of the shoe must be further forwards or further backwards (Figure 72). If the foot and the shoe folding line are not in the same place, the shoe "works" against the foot [21].

Very painful overloading is common in the arches. It is useless to try to counteract this with flat feet pads or insoles. This is the result of more than ten years' of analysis by the author of suitable and unsuitable running shoes for a female runner with short toes and spread feet. This is known to hardly any shoe-buyers and only very few experts despite being published several times!

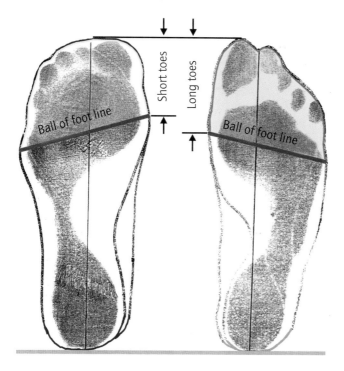

Figure 71: The rear foot is the same length for both runners, but the toes are clearly of different lengths. These differences must be considered when buying shoes. For short toes (left) a running shoe with a far forward folding line is needed. For the right one the fold line must be further back (see Figure 72).

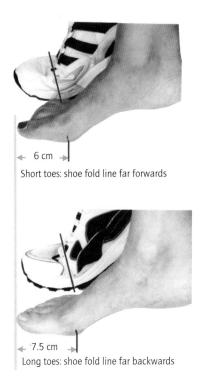

Figure 72: Top: The fold line must be far forwards to suit the short toes.
Bottom: The folding line lies further back to suit the toes.

6 cm
Short toes: shoe fold line far forwards

7.5 cm
Long toes: shoe fold line far backwards

The establishing of the shoe fold line is easy in theory. Hold the shoe horizontally in the open hands and push the hands slightly towards each other. The sole of the shoe folds on its fold line.

9.2.4.3 Shoe Length

N.B. There are no established norms or standards for the sizes and widths of sports shoes. Shoe sizes are "house numbers" – they are usually given as one or two sizes smaller than normal street shoes! The practice is worse: The sizes do not only vary from one manufacturer to another, but also from model to model from the same manufacturer. Women should therefore not be surprised if the running shoe that fits them is two sizes larger than their street shoes.

To find the correct length, take out the inner sole and place the foot on it. There should still be about 1 cm of room at the end of the longest toe.

It is better to try on new running shoes in the afternoon. The feet are bigger at this time than in the morning. Inside the shoe there must be at least (!) one thumb's width (1cm) at the end of the toes, so that the foot can slide forwards unhindered as it unwinds (Figure 73).

Blue toenails are the consequence of lack of space and a visible sign of shoes that are too short. Shoes that are too short, particularly in childhood and adolescence, cause flat feet. Even today, every other child wears shoes that are 1-2 sizes too small without complaining. The child's foot is so weak that it adapts easily, but flat feet are the result.

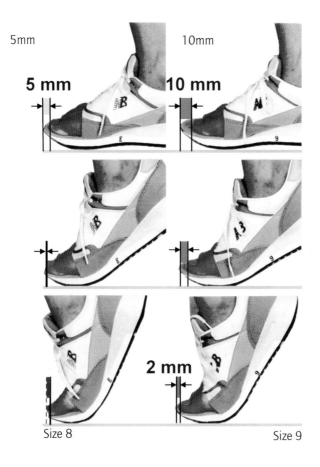

Figure 73: Left: *With only 5mm of free space, as the foot unrolls, it slides so far forwards that the toes stick out 2mm over the tip of the shoe and in a normal case push against the toecap.*
Right: *The toes have enough room and can slide forwards without being squashed.*

9.2.4.4 Toe Room and Shoe Width

The width must be as correct as the length. The forefootand the toes in particular need sufficient space regarding width, too. On the other hand, the shoe must fit tightly in the middle foot area. This is why one manufactures, New Balance, offers shoes of different widths (Figure 74). With all other manufactures runners must put the shoes on to find out whether they are narrow or wide. For a lot of models the following holds true: They are too wide for Middle-Europeans.

Width 2A   Width D   Width 2A: yellow
Width D: yellow + green

Figure 74:
Left: In a 2A width shoe this slim foot finds optimal fit.
Centre: For the same foot D width is clearly too wide.
Right: The yellow area shows the volume of the toe box of the 2A width shoe, while the green area shows the additional volume provided by D width.

9.2.4.5 Heel Position and Support

The heels should fit impeccably from the outset. The foot is controlled from the heel. If the heel is not held correctly, the foot can move about inside the shoe. Tight lacing can only just about correct a badly fitting heel. You should beware of very hard heel caps, which are always in fashion. They can cause painful pressure points for runners with very strongly developed heel bones. The test in Figure 75 shows whether or not the heel fits well.

Figure 75: Heel fit test. Tie the laces correctly. With the right shoe, hold the left shoe on the ground and try to slip the left foot out of the laced shoe. Then repeat with the other foot.

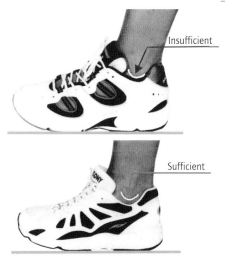

Insufficient

Sufficient

Figure 76: Ankle freedom. The gap between the bottom of the ankle joint and the shoe should be at least 3 mm.

9.2.4.6 Ankle Freedom

Insufficient ankle freedom is one of the hidden defects. It affects the smaller ladies' models more frequently than the larger mens' shoes. There is enough ankle freedom if the gap between the bottom of the ankle joint and the shoe is 3 mm. If it is smaller, you should take out the insole to test whether the ankle touches the side of the shoe. If it does, there is a danger that this painful contact could occur after running a few kilometres, when the cellular structure of the foam insole is compacted.

9.2.4.7 Lacing

The shoe controls the foot (see Chapter 9.1.2.1 "Controlling"). This task can only be carried out effectively if the fit of the foot is ensured by correct lacing. In a badly laced shoe the foot slides about and can't get a grip, which inevitably leads to overloading of tendons, ligaments, muscles and joints. On umpteen occasions the author has just had to tighten lacing to eliminate foot pain in the context of his running shoe advisory work

Conventional hole lacing allows the most individual lacing styles. Ghilly lacing with the big plastic eyelets is simple and faster to handle – but in the case of a high instep it can cause problems.

For many foot forms it can be desirable to lace at different tightnesses in the forefoot and the foot arch area. A dividing knot (see Figure 77) enables this to be done easily.

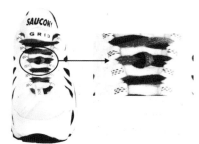

Figure 77: The dividing knot.

9.2.5   Advice, Treadmill Test, Orthotics

Few sports shops offer qualified advice, and they are not widely known. General recommendations are not possible. The runner will only know whether a shoe that feels good on the foot in the shop actually fits when he has worn for one or two hours. If there is one available, it can be a good idea to run on a treadmill for at least half an hour, better still one hour.

Checking the support quality of a shoe on the treadmill is always a valuable help. It requires a lot of experience and is only worthwhile in conjunction with slow-motion video analysis. Without the latter it is of little use.

NB: These days, over-pronation can even be corrected without orthotics with the wide variety of stabilising shoes (see Figure 66). Orthopaedic orthotics are still necessary for flat feet, **which must be fitted as whole-foot insoles in the running shoe.** The correct location of the flat foot pad is also not always found by the specialist in the first fitting; a second or third correction may be necessary.

9.2.6   Experience with previous Running Shoes

"New" means the unknown and risk. "Tried and tested" means building on good experiences. The latter – particularly for runners with foot problems – means going back to running shoes and lasts with which you have had good experiences. This can avoid many expensive mistaken purchases.

9.2.7   Price

Today there are around 300 models of running shoe on the market, i.e. shoes that have already been manufactured. There are also a similarly large number of so-called discontinued models. Companies always declare their discontinued models very reluctantly, as they involve cutting prices.

Nowadays, running shoes cost at least 75 $/50 £ and up to 150 $/100 £. Price does not always mean quality, though. Expensive shoes can be better, but are not necessarily so. Often they are just a status symbol/fashion statement for the wearer or the manufacturer.

At the cheaper end of the scale, there are two or three different groups. At the lowest prices, below 60 $/40 £, there are very few models suitable for running. In the discontinued models at reduced prices there are many bargains but also unsuitable models. Not every cheap running shoe is good value!

10   Bibliography

1.   Ahonen, J./Lathinen, T./Sandström, M./Pogliani, G./Wirhed, R.: Sportmedizin und Trainingslehre. Schattauer Verlag, Stuttgart (1994).
2.   Aigner, A. (Hrsg.): Sportmedizin in der Praxis. Springer-Verlag, Berlin (1986).
3.   Amaling, H.: Aquajogging. In: Betrifft Sport – Lehr- und Lernhilfen für Sportlehrer und Übungsleiter 3/2000, 12-26.
4.   Appel, H.-J./Stang-Voss, C.: Funktionelle Anatomie. Bergmann Verlag, München (1986).
5.   Baum, K.: Krafttraining bei Senioren: Hilfe zum Leben im Alter. In: Dtsch. Z. Sportmed. 4/1995, 214-219.
6.   Beneke, R./Leithäuser, R. M./Schwarz, V./Heck, H.: Maximales Laktat-Steady-State bei Kindern und Erwachsenen. In: Dtsch. Z. Sportmed. 3/2000, 100-104.
7.   Benner, K. U.: Atlas der Anatomie. Bechtermünz Verlag Augsburg (1997).
8.   Beyer, H./Walter W. (Hrsg.): Lehrbuch der organischen Chemie. 19. Aufl., S. Hirzel Verlag, Stuttgart (1981).
9.   Bleicher, A./Mader, A./Mester, J.: Eine Methode zur Approximation der maximalen Laktatbildungsrate und ihre Bedeutung für Stufentests. Symp. Forschungsmeth. Aspekte von Bewegung, Motorik und Training im Sport. Damstadt, 17.-19.9.98.
10.   Böning, D.: Muskelkater – Ursachen, Vorbeugen, Behandlung. In: Dtsch. Z. Sportmed. Sonderheft 1988, 4-7.
11.   Böning, D.: Muskelkater. In: Dtsch. Z. Sportmed. 2/2000, 63-64.
12.   Brouns, F.: Sportler Getränke – Wider diese pseudowiss. Irrmeinungen! In: Arzt+Sport Nr. 2 (4/1992) 26-35.
13.   Cavanagh, P.: The Biomechanics of Distance Running. Human Kinetics Publisher Champaign, Illinois (1990).
14.   Conzelmann, A.: Entwicklung motorischer Fähigkeiten im Lebenslauf – aktuelle Themen. In: Dtsch. Z. Sportmed. Sonderheft 1/1998, 310-315.
15.   Conzelmann, A.: Zur Entwicklung der Ausdauerleistungsfähigkeit im Alter. In: Sportwissenschaft 2/1988, 160-175.
16.   Czioska, F.: Der optimale Laufschuh. Meyer & Meyer Verlag, Aachen (2000).
17.   Diem, C.: Ozon - oben zu wenig, unten zu viel. In: Triathlon & Duathlon 3/1994, 53-54.
18.   Diem, C.-J.: Umfrageanalyse bei 510 LAUF-TREFF-TeilnehmernInnen. Alle Daten beim Verfasser, nur z.T. veröffentlicht (1993).
19.   Diem, C.-J.: Testkriterien für Lauf-(Jogging-)Schuhe: In: Sportverl. Sportschaden 4/1993, 196-199, Georg Thieme Verlag, Stuttgart.

20. Diem, C.-J.: Tipps für Laufanfänger. 6. überarbeitete Aufl., Meyer & Meyer Verlag, Aachen (2000).

21. Diem, C.-J./Lang, D.: Die dritte Dimension. In: SportSpezial-CONDITION 10/1992, 8-14.

22. Diem, C.-J./Hess, H.: Der Laufschuh-Ratgeber. Sportinform Verlag, Oberhaching (1986).

23. Diem, C.-J./Schwebel, W.: Gesundheitsförderung durch Lauftherapie – Welche Möglichkeiten bietet der LAUF-TREFF? In: Alexander Weber (Hrsg.): Hilf dir selbst: Laufe, 100-114, Jungfermann Verlag, Paderborn (1999).

24. Fassbender, H. G.: Osteoarthrose oder Osteoarthritis? In: Colloquia Rheumatologica 21– Aktuelle Rheumaprobleme 20-36, Werk-Verlag Dr. Edmund Banaschewski, München (1984).

25. Fieser, L. F./Fieser, M.: Lehrbuch der organischen Chemie. 4. Aufl., Verlag Chemie, Weinheim (1960).

26. Gabriel, H./Kindermann, W.: Immunsystem und körperliche Belastung: Was ist gesichert? In: Dtsch. Z. Sportmed. Sonderheft 1/1998, 93-99.

27. Hanafi, H. et. al.: Ausgewählte Stretchingübungen für Mittel-/Langstreckenläufer. In: Leichtathletik 48/1986, 1535-1538; 49/1986, 1567-1570.

28. Hartmann, S./Bung, P./Platten, P./Rost, R.: Sport und Schwangerschaft. In: Dtsch. Z. Sportmed. 7-8/1997, 282-289

29. Heck, H./Mader, A./Müller, R./Hollmann, W.: Laktatschwellen und Trainingsteuerung. In: Dtsch. Z. Sportmed., Sonderheft 1996, 72-78.

30. Heck, H./Rosskopf, P.: Die Laktat-Leistungsdiagnostik – valider ohne Schwellenkonzepte. In: TW Sport+Medizin 5/1993, 344-352.

31. Hessisches Ministerium für Jugend, Familie und Gesundheit: Ozon. Referat Presse und Öffentlichkeitsarbeit Wiesbaden (1992).

32. Hof-Mussler, S.: Sport und Immunsystem. In: Med. Mo. Pharm. 12/1991, 362-363

33. Hoffmann, G.: Eisenstoffwechsel der Frau im Sport. In: Dtsch. Z. Sportmed. 5/1998, 173-174.

34. Hollmann, W.: Lebensverlängerung durch sportliche Aktivität. In: Spektrum der Wissenschaft 10/1987, 22-28.

35. Hollmann, W.: Definitionen und Grundlagen zur Trainingslehre. In: Dtsch. Z. Sportmed. 9/1993, 83-389.

36. Hollmann, W.: Ozon: ein Sportkiller. In: Die Fitmacher 3/1993, 5.

37. Hollmann, W./Strüder, K. H.: Das menschliche Gehirn als Agitator und Rezeptor von muskulärer Arbeit. In: Dtsch. Z. Sportmed. Sonderheft 1/1998, 154-160.

38. HolLmann, W./Hettinger, T.: Sportmedizin - Arbeits- und Trainingsgrundlagen. 3. Aufl. (Studienausgabe) Schattauer Verlag, Stuttgart (1990).

39. Israel, S./Freiwald, J./Engelhardt, M.: Zielgerichteter Alterssport – Kraft an erster Stelle. In: TW Sport+Medizin 6/1995, 367-374.
40. Janssen, P. G.: Ausdauertraining – Trainingssteuerung über die HF- und Milchsäurebestimmung. In: Beiträge zur Sportmedizin, Band 34, Perimed Fachbuch-Verlag, Erlangen (1989).
41. Jeschke, D./Heitkamp, H. Ch.: Sportmedizinischer Untersuchungsbefund an Dauerläufern im mittleren Alter. Manuskript (1987 ?) – Sportmedizin, Uni Tübingen Innere Medizin.
42. Kleinmann, D.: Laufen – Sportmedizinische Grundlagen, Trainingslehre und Risikoprophylaxe. Schattauer Verlag, Stuttgart (1996).
43. Knebel, K. P.: Fitnessgymnastik. rororo-Sport 8636, Reinbeck (1991).
44. Kramarz, S.: Leistungssport und Immunsystem. In: Dtsch. Z. Sportmed. 11-12/1997, 449-452.
45. Kuhnle, O.: Trainingspulsmessungen zur Leistungskontrolle. In: Z. Allg. Med. 1989, 11-15.
46. Lippert, H.: Anatomie, Text und Atlas. 5. Aufl., Urban&Schwarzenberg, München (1989).
47. Magaria, R.: Energiequellen der Muskelarbeit. Sportmedizinische Schriftenreihe der Deutschen Sporthochschule Leipzig Bd. 13, Johann Ambrosius Barth, Leipzig (1982).
48. Marées, H. de: Sportphysiologie. 8. Aufl., Sport & Buch Strauß, Köln (1996).
49. Markworth, P.: Sportmedizin – Physiologische Grundlagen. rororo Sport Nr. 17049, Rowolth Taschenbuch Verlag, Reinbeck (1998).
50. Moeller, H./Niess, A. M.: Getränke im Sport. In: Dtsch. Z. Sportmed. 9/1997, 360-365.
51. Mörl, H. (Hrsg.): Muskelkrämpfe. Springer-Verlag, Heidelberg (1986).
52. Neumann, G.: Marathon, eine Stoffwechsel-Disziplin. In: Spiridon 7/1990, 19-22.
53. Neumann, G.: Laktatorientiertes Ausdauertraining – Grenzen erkennen, valide Möglichkeiten nutzen. In: TW Sport+Medizin 6/1993, 417-424.
54. Neumann, G.: Regeneration, welchen Wert haben Erholungsphasen für den Sportler? In: Sports Care 3/1997, 2-3.
55. Nigg, B.: Biomechanics of Running Shoes. Human Kinetics Publisher, Champain/Illinois (1986).
56. Nigg, B./Luethi, S.: Bewegungsanalysen beim Laufschuh. Sportwissenschaft 3/1980, 309-320.
57. Nilsson , L.: Eine Reise in das Innere unseres Körpers. Rasch und Röhrig Verlag, Hamburg (1987).
58. Peil, J. M./Schröder, U./Wagner, P.: Mineralwasser im Vergleich: Welche sind läufergerecht? In: Spiridon 4/1995, 26.

59. Peters, C./Mucha, C./Michna, H./Lötzerich, H.: Vergleichende Untersuchung zum Immunstatus trainierter und untrainierter Junioren und Senioren. In: Dtsch. Z. Sportmed. Sonderheft 1/1998, 111-114.
60. Randall, H.: Schwerpunktsanalyse von Unfällen beim Freizeitsport „Joggen". Diplomarbeit J. W. Goethe-Universität Frankfurt, Herbst 1994.
61. Reinhardt, L./Wuster, K. G.: Sportliche Belastung bei einer Schwangerschaft. In: Dtsch. Z. Sportmed. 2/1995, 132-133.
62. Rost, R.: Das Sportherz. In: Z. Allg. Med. 1988, 239-248.
63. Saziorski, W. M./Aljeschinski, S. J./Jakunin, N. A.: Biomechanische Grundlagen der Ausdauer. Sportverlag Berlin (1987).
64. Schlemmer, W./Schmitt, M.: Sportmedizin und Pharmazie. Wissenschaftliche Verlagsgesellschaft, Stuttgart (1990).
65. Schlumberger, A./Hemmling, G./Frick, U./Schmidtbleicher, D.: Herzfrequenz- und Laktatverhalten beim freien Laufen und beim Aquajogging. In: Dtsch. Z. Sportmed. 5/1997, 183-189.
66. Schmidt, M./Klümper, A.: Basisgymnastik für Jedermann. Reba-Verlag, Darmstadt (1989).
67. Schnack, G.: Intensivstretching und Ausgleichsgymnastik. Deutscher Ärzte-Verlag, Köln (1992).
68. Schnack, G.: Intensivstretching für Jogger. In: Dtsch. Z. Sportmed. 5/1997, 202-206.
69. Segesser, B./Nigg, B.: Orthopädische und biomechanische Konzepte im Sportschuhbau. In: Sportverl. Sportschaden 7/1993, 150-162.
70. Shephard, R. J./Shek, P. N.: Richtig dosiertes Training – auch im Alter eine Hilfe für das Immunsystem. In: Dtsch. Z. Sportmed. 5/1995, 283.
71. Strauss, R. H. (Hrsg.): Sportmedizin und Leistungsphysiologie. Enke Verlag, Stuttgart (1983).
72. Strunz, T.: Mentales Training – man muß wollen, was man will!. In: Arzt+Sport-Spezial Mineralstoff-Symposium 20.06.92, 32-35.
73. Stüssi, E./Stacoff, A./Lucchinetti, E.: Dämpfung versus Stabilität. In: Sportverl. Sportschaden 7/1993, 167-170.
74. Thews, G./Mutschler, E./Vaupel, P.: Anatomie, Physiologie, Pathophysiologie des Menschen. 3. Aufl., Wissenschaftliche Verlagsgesellschaft, Stuttgart (1989).
75. Tittel, K.: Beschreibende und funktionelle Anatomie des Menschen. 8. Aufl., VEB Fischer Verlag, Jena (1978).
76. Weber, A.: „Ich fühle mich unglaublich wohl" – Warum Läufer laufen. In: Herz & Gesundheit 4/1981, 17-19.
77. Weber, A. (Hrsg.): Hilf dir selbst: Laufe!. (Kongreß: Gesundheitsförd. durch Lauftherapie, Bad Lippspringe, 18-20.4.97), Jungfermann Verlag, Paderborn (1999).

78.   Weizt, B.: Atlas der Anatomie. Weltbild Verlag, München (1998).
79.   Wolpert, W./Becker, G.: Der Einfluß muskulärer Dysbalancen auf die Verletzungsanfälligkeit. In: Krankengymnastik 8/1997, 1311-1316.

Photo & Illustration Credits

Cover design: Jens Vogelsang
Illustrations: Carl-Jürgen Diem
Cover photo: Stefan Eisend & Polar Electro
Photos (interior):   Carl-Jürgen Diem & Polar Electro

Lydiard/Gilmour
Jogging with Lydiard

Lydiard/Gilmour
Running with Lydiard

This book renews Arthur Lydiard's philosophy of jogging, just as it was 40 years ago. It is your guide to why you should jog, if you are not jogging already; how you jog, or jog better if you jog already; how it holds back the degeneration that does not necessarily have to accompany the advancing years. Jogging will not stop you growing older but it will help you to grow older more gracefully and with less loss of both physical and mental mobility.

Since the outstanding success of his New Zealand athletes Snell, Halberg and Magee at the 1960 Rome Olympics, Arthur Lydiard's name has been synonymous with the best training methods used by the world's top middle and long-distance runners. His schedules precipitated an athletic revolution, stressing as they did physiological conditioning as the means of achieving this. Running with Lydiard contains expanded information on exercise physiology, diet, injury prevention and cure, discussion of Lydiard's methods and revised training schedules.

104 pages, 10 photos, 1 figure
Two-color print
Paperback, 5^3/4" x 8^1/4"
ISBN 1-84126-070-3
£ 9.95 UK/$ 14.95 US
$ 20.95 CDN/€ 14.90

208 pages, 29 photos, 1 figure
Paperback, 5^3/4" x 8^1/4"
ISBN 1-84126-026-6
£ 12.95 UK/$ 17.95 US
$ 25.95 CDN/€ 18.90

MEYER & MEYER Sport | sales@m-m-sports.com | www.m-m-sports.com

Carl-Jürgen Diem
**Tips for Success –
Running for Beginners**

This book gives the running beginner helpful hints for all questions related to running. It offers information about the form and volume of training as well as clothing and nutrition, and is also a good source of advice for the more experienced runner. It gives practical advice for all those who want to start running as well as for coaches and instructors.

104 pages
Two-color print
61 figures, 1 table
Paperback, 4 ^{1}/2″ x 7″
ISBN 1-84126-072-X
£ 6.95 UK/$ 9.95 US
$ 12.95 CDN/€ 9.90

Petracic/Röttgermann/
Traenckner
Successful Running

"Successful Running" advises on how to improve performance while avoiding physical injury and trauma. This book provides runners with general knowledge to aid self-assessment of individual biological and bio-mechanical problems and over come common overuse injuries. Hence, athletes are in a position to responsibly and consistently counteract problems in good time, facilitating successful and speedy further pursuit of their sport.

144 pages, 11 tables, 180 figures
Paperback, 5 ^{3}/4″ x 8 ^{1}/4″
ISBN 1-84126-006-1
£ 9.95 UK/$ 14.95 US
$ 20.95 CDN/€ 14.90

MEYER & MEYER Sport | sales@m-m-sports.com | www.m-m-sports.com

MEYER
&MEYER
SPORT

Lydiard/Gilmour
**Distance Training
for Masters**

Lydiard/Gilmour
**Distance Training
for Women Athletes**

Lydiard/Gilmour
**Distance Training
for Young Athletes**

136 pages
60 photos
Paperback, 5^3/4″ x 8^1/4″
ISBN 1-84126-018-5
£ 12.95 UK/$ 17.95 US
$ 25.95 CDN/€ 16.90

128 pages
43 photos
Paperback, 5^3/4″ x 8^1/4″
ISBN 1-84126-002-9
£ 9.95 UK/$ 14.95 US
$ 20.95 CDN/€ 14.90

112 pages
78 photos
Paperback, 5^3/4″ x 8^1/4″
ISBN 3-89124-533-5
£ 9.95 UK/$ 14.95 US
$ 20.95 CDN/€ 14.90

Anz running 1/04

MEYER & MEYER Sport | sales@m-m-sports.com | www.m-m-sports.com

Seppo Luhtala (Ed.)
**Top Distance Runners
of the Century**
Motivation, Pain, Success:
World-class Athletes Tell

In this book the greatest stars of distance running openly reveal their vast experience for the young generation. This book is a vital addition to ordinary training manuals and brings human substance to the mechanical part of training. It is a literary source of inspiration for the training process as told by the leading experts of the field – the runners themselves.

360 pages
Full-color print
145 photos
Hardcover, 5^3/4" x 8^1/4"
ISBN 1-84126-069-X
£ 17.95 UK/$ 29.00 US
$ 39.95 CDN/€ 23,90

Arthur Lydiard
Running to the Top

In this book Arthur Lydiard presents an overview of the techniques of middle and long distance running. His description of a systematic, detailed training programme for beginners and top-runners is based on a clear defined conception of fitness. Beneath detailed schedules for training, the book includes tips concerning equipment, kit, nutrition, prevention of injury, therapy and the relationship between the coach and the athlete.

2nd Edition
184 pages, tables
Paperback, 5^3/4" x 8^1/4"
ISBN 3-89124-440-1
£ 12.95 UK/$ 17.95 US
$ 25.95 CDN/€ 16.90

MEYER & MEYER Sport | sales@m-m-sports.com | www.m-m-sports.com

MEYER
& MEYER
SPORT